OSINT: The Ultimate Handbook for Cyber Sleuths

Yevgeny Smirnov

Yevgeny Smirnov is a cybersecurity expert, OSINT (Open Source Intelligence) analyst, and seasoned investigator with over a decade of experience in tracking, analyzing, and neutralizing cyber threats. With a career spanning various sectors—including law enforcement, corporate security, and private intelligence—Yevgeny has developed a unique expertise in utilizing OSINT techniques to uncover hidden connections, mitigate risks, and support investigations worldwide. His work has aided high-profile cases in combating cybercrime, data breaches, and misinformation.

A passionate advocate for open-source intelligence, Yevgeny is committed to empowering individuals and organizations with the knowledge and tools needed to protect themselves in an increasingly interconnected world. His background in cybersecurity and digital forensics, combined with his extensive fieldwork, has positioned him as a trusted authority in the OSINT community. He has delivered training sessions and workshops for security professionals, journalists, and analysts across the globe, sharing his insights on the ethical and effective use of open data.

OSINT: The Ultimate Handbook for Cyber Sleuths is Yevgeny's comprehensive guide for anyone looking to harness the power of open-source intelligence. In this book, he distills years of experience and lessons learned in the field, making it accessible for both newcomers and seasoned professionals. Through practical advice, real-world case studies, and a deep dive into OSINT tools, Yevgeny invites readers to step into the world of cyber sleuthing with confidence, knowledge, and respect for the ethical boundaries of modern intelligence.

In an era where data is omnipresent and open sources contain unprecedented amounts of information, Open Source Intelligence (OSINT) has emerged as an indispensable tool for investigators, cybersecurity professionals, journalists, and analysts. Whether tracking cybercriminals, verifying news, or protecting a company's digital assets, OSINT enables us to connect the dots between seemingly unrelated pieces of data, uncovering hidden patterns and critical insights. However, mastering OSINT isn't merely about using tools; it's about understanding the methods, ethics, and techniques that transform raw data into actionable intelligence.

OSINT: The Ultimate Handbook for Cyber Sleuths is designed as a practical guide for anyone interested in harnessing the power of open data. From beginners looking to understand the basics to experienced analysts who want to refine their skills, this book covers every aspect of OSINT—providing tools, techniques, and case studies that bring the field to life. The chapters are structured to guide readers through every essential area of OSINT, from social media intelligence and geolocation to investigating domains and analyzing digital footprints. By the end, readers will have both the knowledge and confidence to apply OSINT methods ethically and effectively in real-world scenarios.

Chapter 1: Introduction to OSINT and the Power of Open Data

This foundational chapter defines OSINT, explores its evolution, and highlights its role in today's digital world. It also covers the ethical and legal considerations crucial for responsible OSINT use.

Chapter 2: Essential Tools for OSINT Gathering

Introduces the most important tools for OSINT collection and guides readers in selecting the right tool for specific objectives. This chapter also discusses automation techniques that streamline data gathering.

Chapter 3: Social Media Intelligence (SOCMINT)

A deep dive into social media intelligence, this chapter covers techniques for gathering data from platforms like Twitter, Facebook, and LinkedIn. Readers learn to identify real profiles, connections, and understand the ethical boundaries of social media surveillance.

Chapter 4: Geo-Location and Tracking Techniques

Focused on location-based intelligence, this chapter explains how to analyze metadata and use tools like Google Earth to determine locations. Real-world examples illustrate the power of geolocation in investigations.

Chapter 5: Analyzing Digital Footprints

This chapter covers methods for building digital profiles and understanding individuals' online behavior. Readers also learn techniques to protect their own digital footprint, an essential skill for any cyber sleuth.

Chapter 6: Investigating Domains, Websites, and IPs

Domain and IP analysis is key to tracing online activity. This chapter introduces WHOIS databases, reverse IP lookups, and domain analysis techniques that reveal connections between websites and their owners.

Chapter 7: OSINT and Cybercrime Investigation

Explores OSINT's role in tracking cybercriminals and investigating cyber threats. Real-world case studies show how OSINT helps uncover phishing schemes, fraud, and malicious online activities.

Chapter 8: Data Collection from the Deep and Dark Web

This chapter demystifies the deep and dark web, covering tools and precautions for safe exploration. It also examines ethical and legal issues when using data from hidden sources.

Chapter 9: Automated Data Mining and Scripting for OSINT

Covers scripting basics for OSINT, including Python for data automation and web scraping. Readers learn about APIs and how to use them to collect data efficiently, opening up new avenues for data mining.

Chapter 10: Analyzing and Visualizing OSINT Data

Explains how to analyze and visualize collected data to make sense of complex connections. Tools and techniques for creating clear, visual intelligence reports are also discussed.

Chapter 11: Case Studies and Real-World OSINT Applications

This chapter showcases OSINT in action, with case studies from law enforcement, corporate security, and media investigations. Each case highlights techniques and lessons that are invaluable for OSINT practitioners.

Chapter 12: Becoming a Cyber Sleuth: Careers and Skills in OSINT

The final chapter provides insights into pursuing a career in OSINT, including essential skills, certifications, and resources. It also explores the challenges and evolving landscape of open-source intelligence.

Through OSINT: The Ultimate Handbook for Cyber Sleuths, readers will gain a complete understanding of OSINT, equipping them with the skills to gather, analyze, and protect data ethically and effectively. Whether you're a cybersecurity professional, journalist, or an enthusiast aiming to understand the world of cyber sleuthing, this book offers the ultimate roadmap to mastering OSINT.

Chapter 1: Introduction to OSINT and the Power of Open Data

Chapter 1, Introduction to OSINT and the Power of Open Data, provides a foundational understanding of Open Source Intelligence (OSINT) and its critical role in today's digital landscape. It explains OSINT as the process of gathering publicly available information from diverse online and offline sources to create actionable insights. The chapter covers the evolution of OSINT from traditional intelligence methods, highlights its ethical and legal considerations, and introduces the various types of data OSINT specialists leverage—from public records and social media to dark web sources. This introduction sets the stage for readers to appreciate the vast potential and responsibility inherent in using open data for cybersecurity, investigation, and research.

1.1 Understanding Open Source Intelligence (OSINT): Defining OSINT, its evolution, and how it fits into cybersecurity and intelligence.

Open Source Intelligence (OSINT) refers to the collection, analysis, and dissemination of information gathered from publicly available sources. This includes a wide range of materials such as news articles, social media posts, public records, websites, and more. Unlike classified intelligence, which is often obtained through covert methods and is restricted to a select group of individuals or agencies, OSINT is accessible to anyone with an internet connection or access to public resources.

OSINT is distinguished from other forms of intelligence primarily by its sources. The information must be publicly available and legally obtained. This transparency not only allows for broader participation in intelligence-gathering activities but also places a greater emphasis on ethical considerations and responsible usage. Practitioners of OSINT often include journalists, private investigators, security professionals, and government agencies, all leveraging open data to inform their decisions and actions.

The Evolution of OSINT

The concept of OSINT is not new; its roots can be traced back to traditional intelligence practices. However, the evolution of the internet and digital communication has dramatically transformed how OSINT is collected and utilized.

Historical Context: Historically, intelligence agencies relied on reports from informants, human intelligence (HUMINT), and signals intelligence (SIGINT). While publicly available information played a role, it was often overshadowed by classified data sources. The rise of mass media in the 20th century began to shift this dynamic, as newspapers, radio, and television provided more accessible avenues for information gathering.

Digital Revolution: The advent of the internet in the late 20th century marked a significant turning point for OSINT. The explosive growth of online content, coupled with the rise of social media, changed the landscape of information availability. Today, millions of individuals and organizations share news, opinions, and data online, creating a vast pool of resources for OSINT practitioners to draw from.

OSINT as a Discipline: As the volume of available data grew, so did the need for structured approaches to analyze and synthesize information. The establishment of formal methodologies, tools, and training programs has led to the recognition of OSINT as a distinct discipline within the broader field of intelligence. Organizations began developing frameworks and best practices for effective OSINT gathering and analysis, which further legitimized its use in various sectors, including national security, corporate investigations, and journalism.

Legitimization and Standardization: In the early 21st century, OSINT began to gain traction as a formal component of intelligence gathering. Government agencies, such as the U.S. Department of Defense and the CIA, started to develop dedicated OSINT teams and resources. The establishment of organizations like the Open Source Enterprise (OSE) and the Global Open Source Intelligence (GOSINT) forum further promoted the standardization and sharing of OSINT practices across agencies and countries.

OSINT in Cybersecurity and Intelligence

As the digital landscape has expanded, OSINT has become an essential component of cybersecurity and intelligence operations. Its relevance can be understood through various dimensions:

Threat Intelligence: In cybersecurity, OSINT is used to gather information about potential threats, vulnerabilities, and attack vectors. By analyzing publicly available data, cybersecurity professionals can identify emerging threats, understand attacker methodologies, and enhance their defensive measures. For example, information shared on forums, blogs, and social media can provide early warnings of new malware or phishing schemes.

Risk Assessment: Organizations leverage OSINT to perform risk assessments by monitoring their digital footprint and understanding how they are perceived online. By analyzing mentions of their brand, products, or services on social media and review sites, companies can identify potential reputational risks and address them proactively.

Incident Response: In the event of a cybersecurity incident, OSINT can play a crucial role in incident response efforts. Analysts can quickly gather information about the nature of the attack, identify affected systems, and assess the broader impact on their organization. This real-time data can inform response strategies and recovery efforts.

Competitive Intelligence: In the corporate world, OSINT is invaluable for competitive analysis. Businesses can gather intelligence on competitors' activities, product launches, and market positioning by monitoring public sources. This information allows companies to make informed strategic decisions and adapt to market changes.

Law Enforcement and National Security: Law enforcement agencies use OSINT to investigate crimes, track criminal networks, and gather evidence for prosecutions. Similarly, national security organizations employ OSINT to monitor potential threats, assess geopolitical developments, and inform policy decisions. The ability to analyze vast amounts of open data enhances situational awareness and supports proactive measures.

Challenges and Considerations

While OSINT offers significant advantages, it also presents unique challenges:

Data Overload: The sheer volume of available data can be overwhelming. Distinguishing relevant information from noise requires skill and sophisticated analytical tools. Practitioners must be adept at filtering and prioritizing data to focus on actionable insights.

Quality and Reliability: Not all open-source information is credible. OSINT practitioners must critically evaluate the reliability of their sources and be aware of the potential for misinformation or disinformation, especially on social media platforms. Ensuring the accuracy of gathered intelligence is paramount to avoid drawing erroneous conclusions.

Ethical and Legal Considerations: Operating within ethical and legal boundaries is essential for OSINT practitioners. The public nature of the data does not exempt analysts from responsible usage. Issues such as privacy concerns, data protection regulations, and the ethical implications of surveillance must be carefully considered.

Evolving Landscape: The landscape of open data is continuously evolving, influenced by changes in technology, regulations, and public sentiment. OSINT practitioners must remain adaptable and proactive in staying abreast of new tools, methodologies, and ethical considerations.

Open Source Intelligence (OSINT) has emerged as a critical tool for cybersecurity and intelligence operations in the modern digital age. Its evolution from traditional intelligence practices to a distinct discipline underscores the importance of publicly available information in decision-making processes across various sectors. As organizations and individuals increasingly recognize the value of OSINT, its applications continue to expand, providing valuable insights and enhancing situational awareness.

By understanding OSINT's definitions, history, and relevance within cybersecurity and intelligence, practitioners can harness its power to navigate the complexities of today's information-rich environment. As we continue to face new challenges and opportunities in the digital landscape, the responsible and effective use of OSINT will remain paramount for those seeking to safeguard information, make informed decisions, and uncover critical insights.

1.2 Legal and Ethical Considerations: Navigating privacy laws, ethical boundaries, and common OSINT regulations.

As Open Source Intelligence (OSINT) becomes increasingly integral to various fields, understanding the legal and ethical landscape surrounding its practice is crucial. The proliferation of publicly available information, coupled with rapid technological advancements, necessitates a careful examination of privacy laws, ethical boundaries, and regulations that govern OSINT activities. This chapter provides a comprehensive overview of these considerations, helping practitioners navigate the complex terrain of OSINT responsibly.

Privacy Laws

Overview of Privacy Legislation: Privacy laws aim to protect individuals' personal information from unauthorized access, use, and disclosure. These laws vary widely across jurisdictions but generally share common principles, such as the need for consent, transparency, and accountability.

General Data Protection Regulation (GDPR): The GDPR is one of the most significant privacy laws affecting OSINT in the European Union (EU) and beyond. It establishes strict guidelines for the collection and processing of personal data, granting individuals greater control over their information. Key provisions include:

- **Consent**: Organizations must obtain explicit consent from individuals before processing their personal data.
- **Right to Access**: Individuals have the right to request access to their data and understand how it is being used.
- **Data Minimization**: Organizations should only collect data that is necessary for the specified purpose.
- **Right to Erasure**: Individuals can request the deletion of their personal data under certain conditions.

Practitioners must be aware that even when collecting information from public sources, they must respect the rights outlined in the GDPR, especially when the data pertains to individuals based in the EU.

Health Insurance Portability and Accountability Act (HIPAA): In the United States, HIPAA governs the use and disclosure of Protected Health Information (PHI). While OSINT may not typically involve health data, practitioners must be cautious when handling any information that could be classified as PHI to avoid legal repercussions.

California Consumer Privacy Act (CCPA): The CCPA provides California residents with rights regarding their personal data, including the right to know what data is being collected, the right to delete it, and the right to opt-out of its sale. OSINT practitioners operating in California or dealing with data from California residents must comply with CCPA provisions.

Ethical Boundaries

Understanding Ethics in OSINT: Ethics in OSINT refers to the moral principles that govern the practice of gathering and analyzing publicly available information. Ethical considerations are paramount in maintaining public trust and ensuring responsible use of data.

Transparency and Integrity: Practitioners should strive for transparency in their methods and intentions. Clearly communicating the purpose of data collection and analysis helps build trust with stakeholders and the public. Ethical OSINT practitioners should avoid manipulating or misrepresenting data to support preconceived narratives.

Respecting Privacy: While OSINT focuses on publicly available information, it is essential to respect the privacy of individuals. Practitioners should avoid intrusive methods of data collection, such as stalking or harassment, even if the information is accessible online. The principle of "do no harm" should guide OSINT practices, ensuring that individuals' rights and dignity are preserved.

Avoiding Malicious Intent: Ethical OSINT practitioners must refrain from using their skills for malicious purposes, such as cyberstalking, harassment, or discrimination. The motivations behind OSINT activities should align with ethical standards and societal values.

Common OSINT Regulations

Legal Frameworks: Various legal frameworks govern the practice of OSINT, depending on the jurisdiction and specific contexts. Familiarity with relevant laws is crucial for OSINT practitioners to avoid legal pitfalls.

Anti-Cyberstalking Laws: Many jurisdictions have laws aimed at preventing cyberstalking and harassment. OSINT practitioners must be aware of these regulations to ensure their activities do not infringe upon individuals' rights or contribute to harassment.

Intellectual Property Laws: Practitioners should also consider intellectual property rights when collecting data. Using copyrighted materials without permission can lead to legal consequences. Proper attribution and respect for intellectual property rights are essential.

Terms of Service and Platform Policies: Each online platform (e.g., social media sites, forums) has its terms of service that outline acceptable usage and data collection practices. OSINT practitioners should review and adhere to these terms to avoid violating platform policies and potentially facing penalties.

Data Protection Authorities: Many countries have data protection authorities responsible for enforcing privacy laws and regulations. Practitioners should stay informed about the guidelines issued by these authorities to ensure compliance with relevant laws.

Best Practices for Ethical OSINT

Establish Clear Guidelines: Organizations engaged in OSINT should develop clear policies and guidelines that outline acceptable practices and ethical considerations.

These guidelines should promote responsible data collection, analysis, and dissemination.

Training and Education: Providing training on legal and ethical considerations is vital for OSINT practitioners. Continuous education helps professionals stay updated on changing laws and ethical standards in the field.

Conduct Ethical Reviews: Before embarking on OSINT projects, practitioners should conduct ethical reviews to evaluate potential risks and ethical dilemmas. This proactive approach can help identify and mitigate ethical concerns before they arise.

Engage with Stakeholders: Practitioners should engage with relevant stakeholders, including legal experts, privacy advocates, and affected individuals, to gain diverse perspectives on ethical considerations. This engagement fosters collaboration and accountability.

Document Decisions: Keeping records of decisions made during the OSINT process can help practitioners demonstrate their commitment to ethical practices and compliance with legal requirements.

Navigating the legal and ethical landscape of Open Source Intelligence is essential for practitioners to ensure responsible and effective data collection and analysis. With the increasing volume of publicly available information and the evolving nature of privacy laws, understanding the implications of OSINT activities is more critical than ever. By adhering to legal requirements, respecting ethical boundaries, and implementing best practices, OSINT practitioners can harness the power of open-source data while upholding public trust and maintaining the integrity of their work. In doing so, they contribute positively to the broader fields of intelligence, cybersecurity, and data analysis, enhancing their ability to inform decisions and drive impactful outcomes.

1.3 The Types of Data OSINT Covers: Exploring public records, social media, dark web sources, and other OSINT data types.

Open Source Intelligence (OSINT) encompasses a diverse array of publicly available information that can be utilized for intelligence gathering, research, and analysis. The richness of OSINT lies in its ability to draw from various sources, each offering unique insights. This chapter explores the different types of data that OSINT covers, including public records, social media, dark web sources, and other valuable information types.

1. Public Records

Public records form the backbone of OSINT, providing foundational information that can be accessed by anyone. These records are typically maintained by government agencies and are often subject to transparency laws that require them to be made available to the public.

Types of Public Records:

- **Vital Records**: This includes birth and death certificates, marriage licenses, and divorce decrees. These documents can help establish identity and familial connections.
- **Property Records**: Information about property ownership, deeds, and tax assessments can be accessed through county assessor's offices or online databases. This data can reveal ownership patterns and potential financial obligations tied to a property.
- **Court Records**: Legal documents such as criminal records, civil cases, and judgments are generally available through court systems. Analyzing court records can provide insights into an individual's legal history and potential affiliations.
- **Business Licenses and Filings**: Information about registered businesses, including ownership and financial disclosures, is often available from state business registries. This data can help analysts understand business relationships and market dynamics.
- **Government Contracts and Grants**: Information on government spending, including contracts and grants awarded to businesses and organizations, can shed light on public funds allocation and influence.
- **Accessing Public Records**: Many public records can be accessed online through government websites, while others may require formal requests under laws like the Freedom of Information Act (FOIA) in the United States. It's essential to know the regulations surrounding access to ensure compliance.

2. Social Media

Social media platforms are rich sources of real-time information and public sentiment, making them invaluable for OSINT. The vast amount of user-generated content on platforms like Facebook, Twitter, LinkedIn, and Instagram can provide insights into individual behaviors, trends, and events.

Types of Social Media Data:

- **User Profiles**: Public profiles can reveal a wealth of information about individuals, including their interests, affiliations, and social networks.
- **Posts and Updates**: Analyzing posts, comments, and interactions can provide insights into public sentiment, trending topics, and community discussions. Social media can also serve as a platform for sharing breaking news.
- **Multimedia Content**: Images and videos posted on social media can be analyzed for metadata (such as location and time stamps) and content analysis, revealing further context about events or individuals.
- **Groups and Events**: Participation in specific groups or events can highlight affiliations and interests, providing additional context for social networks or community engagement.
- **Challenges in Social Media OSINT**: While social media offers a wealth of information, it also presents challenges, such as misinformation, privacy settings that limit access, and the need for careful interpretation of online behavior. Analysts must develop skills to discern credible information from noise and avoid ethical pitfalls.

3. Dark Web Sources

The dark web comprises a portion of the internet that is not indexed by traditional search engines and requires specific software (like Tor) to access. It is often associated with anonymity and illicit activities but also contains valuable information for OSINT practitioners.

Types of Dark Web Data:

- **Forums and Marketplaces**: Various forums and marketplaces on the dark web facilitate discussions and transactions related to illegal goods and services. Monitoring these platforms can provide insights into criminal activities, emerging threats, and the dynamics of underground economies.
- **Leaked Data and Documents**: The dark web is often a repository for stolen data, including personal information, credit card details, and corporate documents. Analysts can track these leaks to assess potential risks to individuals and organizations.
- **Political Activism**: Some sections of the dark web are used for whistleblowing and political activism, providing a platform for individuals to share information

about government misconduct or corporate corruption. This information can be crucial for investigative journalism and advocacy.

- **Navigating the Dark Web**: While the dark web can offer valuable insights, accessing it requires caution and adherence to legal and ethical guidelines. Practitioners must prioritize their security and anonymity while respecting the boundaries of legal frameworks.

4. Other OSINT Data Types

Beyond public records, social media, and the dark web, OSINT encompasses a variety of other data types that can enrich intelligence gathering efforts.

News Media: Traditional news sources, both print and digital, remain vital for OSINT. Journalists often provide context, analysis, and breaking news that can be crucial for situational awareness. Monitoring multiple news outlets allows practitioners to assess media bias and verify information.

Academic and Research Publications: Scholarly articles, research reports, and white papers can offer in-depth analysis and data on specific topics. Academic databases and institutional repositories serve as excellent resources for gathering reliable information.

Geospatial Data: Satellite imagery and mapping services (like Google Maps and OpenStreetMap) can provide geographic context for investigations. Geospatial data can be utilized to track movements, analyze terrain, and monitor changes over time.

Publicly Available Databases: Various organizations maintain databases that provide access to a wide range of information, including crime statistics, economic data, and demographic information. Utilizing these databases can offer valuable insights into social and economic trends.

Blogs and Online Communities: Niche blogs and online forums can provide specialized knowledge and insights into specific industries, hobbies, or communities. Engaging with these platforms allows practitioners to tap into expert opinions and firsthand accounts.

Open Source Intelligence encompasses a vast array of data types that can be leveraged for intelligence gathering and analysis. From public records to social media, dark web sources, and beyond, each type of data offers unique insights and opportunities.

Understanding the strengths and limitations of these various data sources is essential for effective OSINT practice. As practitioners navigate the diverse landscape of open-source data, they must develop the skills to synthesize information from multiple sources, assess credibility, and maintain ethical standards. By doing so, they can enhance their intelligence capabilities and contribute meaningfully to their fields, whether in cybersecurity, law enforcement, corporate analysis, or investigative journalism.

Chapter 2: Essential Tools for OSINT Gathering

Chapter 2, Essential Tools for OSINT Gathering, dives into the indispensable tools that enable effective open-source intelligence collection. This chapter introduces readers to a wide array of OSINT tools, ranging from search engines and browser extensions to specialized software and data aggregation platforms. Each tool is explained in terms of its strengths, limitations, and best use cases, helping readers select the right tools for their specific needs. The chapter also covers the basics of automation, showing how to streamline repetitive data collection tasks to save time and increase efficiency. By the end, readers will have a comprehensive toolkit to enhance their OSINT capabilities, laying a strong foundation for deeper investigative work.

2.1 The OSINT Toolbox: Overview of essential tools like Maltego, Shodan, and Google Dorking.

In the realm of Open Source Intelligence (OSINT), having the right tools at your disposal can significantly enhance the effectiveness and efficiency of your information-gathering efforts. This section provides an overview of some essential OSINT tools, including Maltego, Shodan, and Google Dorking, highlighting their functionalities, use cases, and how they fit into the OSINT landscape.

1. Maltego

Overview: Maltego is a powerful data mining tool designed for link analysis and data visualization. It allows users to uncover relationships between various entities, such as people, organizations, domains, and IP addresses, through a graphical interface.

Key Features:

- **Graphical Representation**: Maltego provides a visual interface that enables users to see connections between different data points in real-time. This makes it easier to identify patterns and relationships that may not be immediately apparent in raw data.
- **Transforms**: The tool utilizes "transforms" to automate data gathering from various online sources. Users can run specific queries to extract data about a particular entity and visualize it within the Maltego graph.

- **Integration with Other Tools**: Maltego can integrate with various data sources and APIs, allowing users to extend its functionality and pull in data from different platforms, including social media, DNS information, and more.

Use Cases:

- **Threat Analysis**: Maltego is widely used in cybersecurity for threat analysis and investigation. Analysts can visualize the connections between threat actors, their infrastructure, and potential victims.
- **Social Network Analysis**: OSINT practitioners can map out relationships between individuals and organizations, helping to identify key players in a specific context, such as a corporate investigation or criminal network.
- **Limitations**: While Maltego is a powerful tool, it may require a learning curve for new users. Additionally, some features and transforms may require a paid license, which could limit access for some practitioners.

2. Shodan

Overview: Shodan is a search engine designed for discovering internet-connected devices and services. Unlike traditional search engines that index web pages, Shodan focuses on the underlying hardware and software running on devices, such as routers, servers, and IoT devices.

Key Features:

- **Device Discovery**: Shodan allows users to search for specific devices based on parameters like location, service, and operating system. This makes it easy to find devices exposed to the internet and potentially vulnerable to attacks.
- **Geolocation Data**: Users can visualize device locations on a map, helping to understand the geographical distribution of certain technologies or vulnerabilities.
- **Data Filters**: Shodan offers advanced filtering options, enabling users to narrow down searches based on criteria such as port numbers, protocols, and device types.

Use Cases:

- **Security Assessments**: Cybersecurity professionals use Shodan to conduct security assessments by identifying vulnerable devices within their network or geographic area. This proactive approach helps organizations mitigate potential risks.

- **Research on IoT Security**: Researchers and analysts can utilize Shodan to study the security landscape of Internet of Things (IoT) devices, identifying common vulnerabilities and exposure points.
- **Limitations**: Shodan's data is reliant on devices being connected to the internet and actively responding to queries. Additionally, while some features are available for free, full access to Shodan's capabilities typically requires a paid subscription.

3. Google Dorking

Overview: Google Dorking refers to the technique of using advanced search operators in Google to uncover specific information and vulnerabilities on websites. This method allows users to perform more targeted searches than standard queries, effectively utilizing Google as a powerful OSINT tool.

Key Features:

- **Advanced Search Operators**: Google Dorking leverages a variety of operators, such as site:, filetype:, and inurl:, to refine searches and retrieve specific types of information. For example, filetype:pdf site:gov would return PDF files hosted on government websites.
- **Vulnerability Discovery**: By crafting specific queries, users can uncover exposed files, configuration errors, and other security vulnerabilities on websites that may not be readily visible through traditional browsing.

Use Cases:

- **Information Gathering**: OSINT practitioners use Google Dorking to collect data from various sources, such as documents, databases, and web pages, that may contain sensitive or useful information.
- **Security Auditing**: Security professionals can employ Google Dorking to identify misconfigurations and vulnerabilities in their own systems or in third-party websites, enabling them to take corrective action.
- **Limitations**: While Google Dorking can be highly effective, it requires knowledge of search operators and may lead to false positives or irrelevant results. Additionally, ethical considerations must be taken into account to avoid violating terms of service or engaging in unauthorized access.

The OSINT toolbox is essential for practitioners aiming to gather and analyze open-source information effectively. Tools like Maltego, Shodan, and Google Dorking provide unique capabilities that enhance the OSINT process, enabling users to visualize relationships, discover vulnerable devices, and uncover hidden information. Understanding the functionalities and applications of these tools is crucial for anyone engaged in OSINT activities, as they significantly contribute to informed decision-making, threat analysis, and strategic planning. By leveraging these essential tools, OSINT practitioners can navigate the complexities of the digital landscape and uncover valuable insights that drive their investigations and analyses.

2.2 Choosing the Right Tool for the Job: How to select the best OSINT tool based on goals and data sources.

In the diverse field of Open Source Intelligence (OSINT), the right tools can make a significant difference in the quality and efficiency of data collection and analysis. However, with a plethora of options available, selecting the appropriate tool can be daunting. This section provides a comprehensive guide on how to choose the right OSINT tool based on your specific goals and the data sources you intend to explore.

1. Define Your Goals

Before diving into the selection process, it's crucial to clearly define your objectives. Understanding what you want to achieve will guide you in choosing the most effective tools. Here are some common goals and considerations:

Information Gathering: Are you looking to collect data about individuals, organizations, or specific events? Tools like Maltego and Google Dorking can help in identifying relationships and gathering information from various online sources.

Threat Assessment: If your focus is on identifying potential threats or vulnerabilities, tools like Shodan may be more suitable. This tool allows you to discover internet-connected devices and assess their security posture.

Social Media Monitoring: For those interested in sentiment analysis or trend tracking, social media-specific tools like TweetDeck or Brandwatch can help gather and analyze data from platforms like Twitter and Instagram.

Investigative Research: If you are conducting investigative research, consider tools that can provide comprehensive data and insights, such as Pipl for deep searches or Social Searcher for social media monitoring.

2. Identify Your Data Sources

The next step in choosing the right OSINT tool involves understanding the data sources relevant to your goals. Different tools excel in extracting data from specific types of sources. Here's a breakdown:

Public Records: If your goal involves accessing public records, tools such as LexisNexis or GovInfo can help you locate government documents, court records, and other publicly available information.

Social Media: For gathering data from social media platforms, specialized tools like Hootsuite for management and monitoring or BuzzSumo for content analysis can provide valuable insights.

Dark Web: If your investigation necessitates access to dark web data, tools like Ahmia or DarkSearch can facilitate searches in this elusive space.

Search Engines: For broad information gathering across the internet, utilizing advanced search operators in Google (Google Dorking) or tools like DuckDuckGo can enhance your search capabilities.

Technical Reconnaissance: If your focus is on understanding technical details about network infrastructure, tools such as Nmap for network mapping or Shodan for device discovery can be highly effective.

3. Assess Tool Features and Capabilities

Once you've defined your goals and identified your data sources, evaluate the specific features and capabilities of potential tools. Here are some considerations:

User Interface: Look for tools with user-friendly interfaces that allow you to navigate easily and access the necessary functionalities without extensive training.

Data Visualization: If analyzing complex relationships or large datasets is crucial for your objectives, tools with strong data visualization capabilities, like Maltego, can help you create clear and informative graphs.

Integration with Other Tools: Some OSINT tools can integrate with other applications or platforms, which can enhance your overall analysis. Check for compatibility and the availability of APIs for seamless data sharing.

Customization and Flexibility: Determine if the tool allows for customization or supports plugins that can enhance its capabilities according to your needs.

Pricing and Licensing: Understand the cost structures associated with the tools. Some tools offer free versions with limited features, while others require subscription fees. Choose a tool that aligns with your budget while providing the necessary features.

4. Consider Legal and Ethical Implications

When selecting OSINT tools, it's essential to consider the legal and ethical implications of their use. Ensure that the tool complies with relevant laws and regulations in your jurisdiction, especially regarding data privacy and usage.

Data Protection Regulations: Familiarize yourself with data protection regulations like the General Data Protection Regulation (GDPR) or the California Consumer Privacy Act (CCPA) to avoid potential legal issues.

Ethical Standards: Adhere to ethical standards in your OSINT practices. Avoid tools that facilitate intrusive or unethical data collection practices, and prioritize those that promote responsible use of information.

5. Test and Evaluate

Before fully committing to a particular OSINT tool, consider conducting trials or pilot projects. Many tools offer free trials or basic versions that allow you to test their functionalities.

Conduct Sample Searches: Perform sample searches relevant to your objectives to evaluate the tool's effectiveness and efficiency in retrieving desired data.

Compare Outputs: If possible, compare outputs from multiple tools to assess which one provides the most relevant and accurate information for your needs.

Gather Feedback: If you are part of a team or organization, gather feedback from colleagues or stakeholders who may also be using the tool. Their insights can provide valuable perspectives on usability and effectiveness.

Choosing the right OSINT tool is a critical step in the intelligence-gathering process. By clearly defining your goals, identifying relevant data sources, assessing tool features, considering legal and ethical implications, and testing options, you can select a tool that best meets your needs. The effectiveness of your OSINT efforts largely depends on the tools you utilize, so investing time in this selection process will enhance your ability to gather meaningful insights, make informed decisions, and achieve your objectives in the ever-evolving landscape of open-source intelligence.

2.3 Automating OSINT Collection: Introduction to automation tools and strategies for efficient data gathering.

As the volume of information available online continues to expand exponentially, the need for efficient data collection in Open Source Intelligence (OSINT) becomes increasingly vital. Automating OSINT collection not only streamlines the process but also enhances the accuracy and speed of data gathering. This section delves into the concept of automation in OSINT, highlighting various tools and strategies that can help practitioners effectively gather and analyze data.

1. The Importance of Automation in OSINT

Automation in OSINT serves several essential purposes:

Efficiency: Manual data collection can be time-consuming and labor-intensive. Automation allows for quicker data retrieval, enabling analysts to focus on higher-level tasks like interpretation and strategy.

Consistency: Automated processes ensure that data collection is conducted uniformly, minimizing human error and enhancing the reliability of the gathered information.

Scalability: Automation makes it feasible to handle large datasets and multiple sources simultaneously, which is particularly beneficial in investigations that require comprehensive data analysis.

Real-Time Monitoring: Automated tools can continuously monitor specified data sources for updates, alerts, and emerging threats, ensuring that analysts receive timely information.

2. Types of Automation Tools

Numerous tools are available for automating OSINT data collection. Below are some notable options across different categories:

Web Scrapers: Tools like Scrapy and Beautiful Soup allow users to extract data from websites efficiently. These tools can automate the retrieval of specific information, such as news articles, social media posts, or public records, by defining parameters and running scripts.

API Integrations: Many online platforms offer APIs (Application Programming Interfaces) that allow automated access to their data. For instance, Twitter's API enables users to collect tweets based on certain criteria, while tools like Postman can facilitate API testing and data extraction from various sources.

Monitoring Tools: Solutions such as Mention and Google Alerts automate the tracking of keywords or topics across the internet. These tools can alert users to relevant new content, helping analysts stay updated on evolving situations or emerging threats.

Data Aggregation Platforms: Tools like Zapier or IFTTT (If This Then That) can connect various applications and automate workflows. For example, a user can set up a workflow that automatically saves tweets containing specific hashtags to a Google Sheet for further analysis.

Custom Scripts: For users with programming knowledge, writing custom scripts in languages like Python or Ruby can facilitate automated data collection. Libraries such as Selenium (for web automation) and Pandas (for data analysis) can be utilized to develop tailored solutions based on specific needs.

3. Strategies for Effective Automation

To maximize the benefits of automation in OSINT, consider the following strategies:

Define Clear Objectives: Clearly outline what information you need and the sources you will target. A well-defined objective will guide the selection of appropriate tools and methodologies for data collection.

Utilize Regular Expressions: Regular expressions (regex) can be employed to filter and extract specific patterns from large datasets. This technique is particularly useful in web scraping, allowing for targeted data retrieval based on defined criteria.

Implement Scheduling and Alerts: Set up automated processes that run on a schedule (daily, weekly, etc.) to ensure continuous data collection. Additionally, configure alerts to notify you of significant changes or new data points relevant to your interests.

Incorporate Data Cleaning: Automated data collection often results in raw data that requires cleaning and preprocessing. Integrate data cleaning scripts to filter out noise, remove duplicates, and standardize formats before analysis.

Prioritize Ethical Considerations: Ensure that your automated data collection processes comply with legal and ethical standards. Familiarize yourself with the terms of service for the platforms you are using and respect privacy laws to avoid potential legal repercussions.

Regularly Review and Optimize: Continuously monitor the performance of your automated systems and adjust as necessary. Review collected data for relevance and accuracy, and be prepared to modify scripts or parameters to improve results.

4. Challenges in Automating OSINT

While automation can significantly enhance OSINT processes, it is not without challenges. Some common issues include:

Rate Limiting: Many platforms impose restrictions on the number of requests that can be made within a specific time frame. Automation scripts should be designed to adhere to these limits to avoid being blocked or banned.

Dynamic Content: Websites that utilize dynamic content (e.g., AJAX) can complicate data scraping efforts. Automation tools must be capable of handling these complexities, requiring more sophisticated approaches to data extraction.

Changing Websites: Websites frequently update their layouts and structures, which can disrupt automated scraping processes. Regular maintenance of automation scripts is necessary to ensure continued functionality.

Data Quality and Validation: Automated data collection may yield inaccurate or low-quality data. Implement validation processes to assess the reliability and credibility of the gathered information before drawing conclusions.

Automating OSINT collection offers a myriad of advantages, including increased efficiency, consistency, and scalability in data gathering. By leveraging various tools and implementing effective strategies, OSINT practitioners can streamline their processes and focus on analyzing the data to inform decision-making. However, it is essential to navigate the challenges and ethical considerations inherent in automation, ensuring compliance with legal standards while maximizing the quality of collected information. As the field of OSINT continues to evolve, automation will play a crucial role in empowering analysts to uncover valuable insights from the vast ocean of open-source data.

Chapter 3: Social Media Intelligence (SOCMINT)

Chapter 3, Social Media Intelligence (SOCMINT), explores techniques for gathering and analyzing intelligence from social media platforms like Twitter, Facebook, LinkedIn, and Instagram. This chapter provides a guide to uncovering user profiles, understanding online connections, and mapping networks based on interactions and content. Readers learn how to monitor public posts, track trends, and extract metadata from social media content while adhering to ethical and legal boundaries. SOCMINT techniques covered here empower readers to reveal hidden relationships and verify information, making it an invaluable tool for investigations, reputation management, and public sentiment analysis.

3.1 Gathering Intelligence from Major Platforms: Techniques for gathering data from Twitter, Facebook, LinkedIn, and Instagram.

In today's digital landscape, social media platforms are rich sources of information, making them valuable tools for Open Source Intelligence (OSINT) practitioners. Each platform offers unique features and data types, allowing users to gather insights into individuals, organizations, and trends. This section outlines techniques for gathering intelligence from four major social media platforms: Twitter, Facebook, LinkedIn, and Instagram.

1. Twitter

Twitter is a fast-paced platform where real-time information flows, making it a treasure trove for OSINT.

Advanced Search: Utilize Twitter's advanced search capabilities to filter tweets based on specific keywords, hashtags, dates, or users. This feature allows practitioners to uncover relevant conversations or trending topics surrounding particular events or individuals.

Twitter API: The Twitter API allows developers to access and analyze large volumes of tweet data programmatically. By using the API, OSINT practitioners can automate data collection, perform sentiment analysis, and track trends over time. Tools like Tweepy (a Python library) can simplify API interactions for data retrieval.

Tweet Analysis Tools: Use specialized tools like TweetDeck for real-time monitoring of specific accounts, hashtags, or keywords. These tools provide a centralized interface to follow multiple conversations simultaneously, enabling practitioners to identify emerging narratives and sentiments.

2. Facebook

Facebook's vast user base and extensive data-sharing capabilities provide an opportunity for detailed intelligence gathering.

Public Profiles: Start by searching for public profiles or pages related to your subject of interest. Pay attention to posts, comments, and interactions to gather insights into personal or organizational activities.

Graph Search: Although Facebook's Graph Search has been limited in functionality, practitioners can still use it to discover connections between individuals, pages, groups, and events. Searching for specific phrases can lead to relevant groups or pages that may not be easily discoverable otherwise.

Content Monitoring: Utilize Facebook's monitoring tools or third-party applications like CrowdTangle to track content engagement metrics. These tools can help analyze trends, popular posts, and user interactions related to specific topics or organizations.

3. LinkedIn

LinkedIn is primarily a professional networking platform, making it ideal for gathering information about individuals' career histories, connections, and industry trends.

Profile Searches: Use LinkedIn's search bar to find profiles based on keywords, job titles, or skills. This method allows OSINT practitioners to gather information about a person's professional background, endorsements, and mutual connections.

Advanced Filters: Leverage LinkedIn's advanced search filters to narrow down results by location, industry, and company. This feature is particularly useful for recruitment investigations, competitive analysis, or organizational mapping.

Content and Group Monitoring: Follow industry-specific groups and discussions to gather insights about market trends, competitor activities, or emerging talents. Tools like LinkedIn Sales Navigator can further enhance lead generation and account tracking capabilities.

4. Instagram

Instagram is a visually oriented platform, making it a valuable resource for understanding brand presence, user engagement, and personal lifestyles.

Hashtag Tracking: Utilize hashtags to discover user-generated content related to specific topics, brands, or events. By following and analyzing these hashtags, practitioners can identify trends, popular influencers, and community sentiments.

Public Accounts and Posts: Explore public profiles to gather insights into user-generated content, location tags, and comments. Analyzing posts and interactions can reveal valuable information about consumer behaviors and preferences.

Third-Party Tools: Consider using social media analytics tools like Hootsuite or Sprout Social to analyze engagement metrics, audience demographics, and content performance on Instagram. These tools can assist in tracking brand mentions and understanding public perception.

Gathering intelligence from major social media platforms like Twitter, Facebook, LinkedIn, and Instagram involves leveraging various techniques tailored to each platform's unique features. By utilizing advanced search functionalities, APIs, content monitoring tools, and analytics platforms, OSINT practitioners can efficiently collect valuable insights from social media. These techniques not only enhance understanding of individuals and organizations but also contribute to broader analyses of trends and public sentiment in the digital age. As social media continues to evolve, staying updated on best practices and emerging tools will remain essential for effective OSINT collection.

3.2 Profiling and Network Mapping: Understanding connections, influence, and networks based on social media interactions.

Social media platforms are not just repositories of individual thoughts and images; they also serve as intricate webs of relationships and influence. Profiling individuals and mapping their networks can provide valuable insights into their connections, influence, and potential behaviors. This section explores techniques for profiling and network mapping based on social media interactions, offering OSINT practitioners the tools needed to analyze relationships effectively.

1. Understanding Profiling in OSINT

Profiling in OSINT involves the collection and analysis of data to create comprehensive profiles of individuals or entities. These profiles often include personal information, interests, affiliations, and behavioral patterns, allowing analysts to gain insights into motivations and potential actions.

Data Points for Profiling: Key data points for creating profiles may include:

- **Demographic Information**: Age, location, education, and occupation derived from social media profiles.
- **Interests and Activities**: Posts, likes, shares, and comments that indicate personal interests or professional affiliations.
- **Connections**: The number and types of connections (friends, followers, etc.) that reveal the individual's network size and reach.
- **Sentiment Analysis**: Use sentiment analysis tools to gauge the emotional tone of an individual's posts and interactions. This can provide insights into their opinions, moods, and potential behaviors.

2. Techniques for Network Mapping

Network mapping involves visualizing relationships between individuals, organizations, and groups based on social media interactions. This process helps identify influential individuals, key connections, and community dynamics.

Graph Visualization Tools: Use tools like Gephi, Cytoscape, or Maltego to create visual representations of networks. These tools allow users to input data about connections and interactions to generate graphs that illustrate relationships.

Social Network Analysis (SNA): SNA techniques can help quantify relationships and interactions. Key metrics include:

- **Degree Centrality**: Measures the number of direct connections an individual has, indicating their immediate influence.
- **Betweenness Centrality**: Identifies individuals who act as bridges between different groups, highlighting their potential as influencers or gatekeepers.
- **Closeness Centrality**: Indicates how quickly an individual can connect to others in the network, suggesting their ability to spread information quickly.

- **Content Interaction Mapping**: Analyze interactions on specific posts (likes, comments, shares) to identify key participants in discussions. Mapping who interacts with whom on specific topics can reveal community leaders and emergent influencers.

3. Analyzing Influence

Understanding influence in social media networks requires examining both qualitative and quantitative aspects of interactions. The following methods can enhance influence analysis:

Follower and Engagement Metrics: Examine the number of followers, likes, shares, and comments to gauge an individual's influence. Tools like BuzzSumo can help analyze the reach and engagement of specific content.

Influencer Identification: Utilize influencer identification tools, such as Upfluence or Klear, to find individuals with significant reach and authority in particular niches. These tools often provide metrics on engagement, audience demographics, and content performance.

Content Analysis: Analyze the type and quality of content shared by individuals to understand their influence. Consider the themes, sentiment, and engagement levels of their posts to determine their authority and credibility within a community.

4. Case Studies and Applications

Profiling and network mapping techniques have numerous applications in various fields, including:

Corporate Intelligence: Companies can utilize these techniques to analyze competitors' networks and identify key personnel within target organizations. This analysis helps in recruitment, partnership strategies, and market positioning.

Crisis Management: In times of crisis, organizations can map public sentiment and influential voices to better understand how information is disseminated and how to respond effectively.

Security and Threat Assessment: Law enforcement and security agencies can use profiling and network mapping to identify potential threats based on social media interactions, recognizing individuals who may have harmful intentions or affiliations.

Market Research: Brands can leverage these techniques to understand consumer behaviors and preferences, helping tailor marketing strategies and product development.

5. Ethical Considerations

While profiling and network mapping can provide significant insights, it is essential to navigate ethical considerations carefully:

Privacy Concerns: Always respect individuals' privacy and comply with relevant laws and regulations regarding data collection and usage. Avoid using deceptive practices to gather information.

Transparency: When presenting findings, ensure that the analysis is transparent and that the methods used to gather data are disclosed. Misrepresenting data can lead to ethical dilemmas and trust issues.

Bias Awareness: Be aware of potential biases in the data and the analysis process. Ensure that conclusions are based on a comprehensive understanding of the context and not on incomplete or skewed data.

Profiling and network mapping based on social media interactions are powerful techniques in the OSINT toolkit. By understanding connections and influence within social networks, analysts can derive meaningful insights that aid in decision-making and strategic planning. As the digital landscape continues to evolve, these methods will become increasingly valuable for understanding complex relationships and dynamics, providing a clearer picture of individuals and their networks in the interconnected world of social media. Careful adherence to ethical considerations will ensure that these powerful techniques are used responsibly and effectively.

3.3 Tools for Social Media Monitoring: Exploring tools like TweetDeck, Social Searcher, and BuzzSumo for SOCMINT.

Social media monitoring is a crucial component of Social Media Intelligence (SOCMINT), allowing analysts to gather insights from the vast amounts of data generated on platforms like Twitter, Facebook, Instagram, and LinkedIn. Effective monitoring tools enable users to track conversations, analyze trends, and gather actionable intelligence. This section will explore three prominent social media monitoring tools—TweetDeck, Social Searcher, and BuzzSumo—highlighting their features, use cases, and benefits for SOCMINT practitioners.

1. TweetDeck

Overview: TweetDeck is a social media dashboard application for managing Twitter accounts. It provides a customizable interface for monitoring multiple Twitter feeds simultaneously, making it an invaluable tool for real-time engagement and analysis.

Key Features:

- **Multiple Column Layout**: Users can set up multiple columns to monitor different Twitter feeds, such as mentions, direct messages, lists, and hashtags. This layout allows for real-time tracking of conversations and trends.
- **Customizable Filters**: TweetDeck enables users to filter tweets based on various criteria, including keywords, user handles, and engagement metrics. This customization helps practitioners focus on relevant conversations.
- **Scheduling Tweets**: Users can schedule tweets to be published at specific times, facilitating consistent engagement with followers without the need for constant monitoring.

Use Cases:

- **Event Monitoring**: TweetDeck is particularly useful during live events (e.g., conferences, product launches) where real-time updates are crucial. Analysts can monitor hashtags and relevant conversations to gather immediate insights.
- **Crisis Management**: During crises, TweetDeck allows organizations to track mentions and sentiment, enabling quick responses to emerging issues or misinformation.
- **Benefits**: TweetDeck's intuitive interface and robust features make it an excellent tool for real-time social media monitoring, allowing practitioners to stay informed and responsive.

2. Social Searcher

Overview: Social Searcher is a comprehensive social media search engine that enables users to monitor public posts across various social media platforms. It aggregates content from platforms such as Twitter, Facebook, Instagram, and Reddit, providing a broad overview of social media discussions.

Key Features:

- **Real-Time Search**: Social Searcher provides real-time monitoring of public posts based on keywords, hashtags, and user handles. This capability enables practitioners to track discussions as they unfold.
- **Sentiment Analysis**: The tool offers sentiment analysis features that help users gauge public opinion around specific topics or brands. This analysis can provide valuable insights into community perceptions and attitudes.
- **Content Aggregation**: Social Searcher aggregates content from multiple platforms, allowing users to view a comprehensive landscape of social media discussions related to their interests.

Use Cases:

- **Brand Monitoring**: Organizations can use Social Searcher to monitor their brand's mentions and understand how they are perceived across social media. This insight can inform marketing strategies and reputation management.
- **Competitor Analysis**: By tracking competitor mentions and conversations, organizations can gain insights into competitors' strategies and public perception, aiding in strategic planning.
- **Benefits**: Social Searcher's multi-platform capabilities and sentiment analysis features make it a powerful tool for gathering diverse insights from social media discussions.

3. BuzzSumo

Overview: BuzzSumo is a content marketing and social media analytics tool that allows users to analyze content performance across social media platforms. It provides insights into trending topics, influential content, and audience engagement metrics.

Key Features:

- **Content Discovery**: Users can discover trending content by searching for specific keywords or topics. BuzzSumo displays the most shared articles, videos, and posts across social media, providing insights into popular themes.
- **Influencer Identification**: BuzzSumo helps users identify key influencers in specific niches. This feature enables practitioners to engage with or leverage these influencers for outreach and content promotion.

- **Engagement Metrics**: The tool provides detailed engagement metrics, including social shares, backlinks, and comments. This information helps users assess the impact and reach of specific content.

Use Cases:

- **Content Strategy Development**: Marketers and content creators can use BuzzSumo to inform their content strategies by identifying popular topics and understanding audience preferences.
- **Competitor Benchmarking**: Organizations can analyze competitors' content performance, revealing insights into what resonates with their audience and helping refine their own strategies.
- **Benefits**: BuzzSumo's focus on content discovery and influencer identification makes it an essential tool for organizations looking to enhance their content marketing efforts and social media presence.

The effective use of social media monitoring tools like TweetDeck, Social Searcher, and BuzzSumo can significantly enhance SOCMINT efforts. These tools offer a range of features for tracking conversations, analyzing sentiment, and understanding trends across social media platforms. By leveraging these resources, OSINT practitioners can gather actionable intelligence, respond to emerging issues, and inform strategic decision-making. As social media continues to evolve, staying updated on the latest monitoring tools and techniques will remain crucial for successful SOCMINT.

Chapter 4: Geo-Location and Tracking Techniques

Chapter 4, Geo-Location and Tracking Techniques, focuses on methods for determining and verifying physical locations through OSINT. Readers learn how to extract and analyze metadata from images, videos, and social media posts to identify geographic coordinates and timestamps. The chapter introduces essential tools like Google Earth, OpenStreetMap, and satellite imagery platforms, explaining how they can be used to corroborate locations and track movements. With real-world examples, this chapter demonstrates the practical applications of geolocation in investigations, from identifying sites of interest to tracking individuals and events across various locations. By mastering these techniques, readers gain powerful skills for pinpointing locations and confirming activities in a variety of investigative contexts.

4.1 Using Metadata for Geolocation: How to extract and analyze metadata from photos and posts to determine location.

Geolocation using metadata is a powerful technique in Open Source Intelligence (OSINT), allowing analysts to pinpoint the location of individuals or events based on the data embedded in digital content. Metadata, the "data about data," provides contextual information about various types of digital files, including photos and posts on social media platforms. This section will explore how to extract and analyze metadata to determine geolocation effectively.

1. Understanding Metadata

Metadata refers to the information that describes other data. In the context of digital media, it can provide insights into the origin, format, and context of files. Common types of metadata include:

EXIF Data: Exchangeable Image File Format (EXIF) data is embedded in images captured by digital cameras and smartphones. This metadata can include camera settings, date and time of capture, and crucially, GPS coordinates (latitude and longitude) if the device has geolocation capabilities enabled.

Social Media Metadata: Posts on platforms like Facebook, Instagram, and Twitter often include metadata such as timestamps, location tags, and user identifiers, which can help determine the geolocation of the content.

Document Metadata: Files such as PDFs or Word documents can contain metadata that provides information about the author, editing history, and sometimes location information if the document was created on a device with GPS capabilities.

2. Extracting Metadata

To utilize metadata for geolocation, analysts first need to extract the relevant information from digital files. Here are methods to do so:

Using EXIF Data Extractors: Tools like ExifTool, PhotoME, or GeoSetter can be used to extract EXIF metadata from image files. These tools provide a comprehensive overview of the metadata, including GPS coordinates if available. To use ExifTool:

Install ExifTool on your system.

- Open the command line and type exiftool image.jpg to extract all metadata from the image file.
- Look for GPSLatitude and GPSLongitude fields, which provide the exact geolocation.

Analyzing Social Media Posts: For social media content, many platforms provide the option to view metadata directly. On Instagram, for instance, users can see the location tagged in a post by tapping on the location name. Alternatively, third-party tools like Social Searcher can aggregate and analyze metadata from various posts.

Document Metadata Extraction: For documents, applications like Apache Tika or DocMetadata can extract metadata from files to uncover any location information or contextual details that may indicate where the document was created or edited.

3. Analyzing Metadata for Geolocation

Once metadata is extracted, the next step is analysis. Here's how analysts can interpret the data to determine location:

Mapping GPS Coordinates: If GPS coordinates are available, they can be plotted on mapping software (e.g., Google Maps, OpenStreetMap) to visualize the exact location.

Analysts can input the latitude and longitude values directly into these mapping applications to view the geolocation on a map.

Reverse Geocoding: In cases where GPS coordinates are available, reverse geocoding can convert the latitude and longitude into a human-readable address. Services like Google Maps Geocoding API or OpenCage Geocoder can be utilized for this purpose, providing valuable context about the location.

Contextual Analysis: Beyond raw GPS data, analysts should consider the broader context of the metadata. For instance, analyzing the date and time of the post or photo can help understand the significance of the location. Additionally, if multiple photos or posts are analyzed, patterns may emerge that indicate frequently visited locations or a person's typical environment.

4. Ethical Considerations

While using metadata for geolocation is a powerful tool for intelligence gathering, ethical considerations must be taken into account:

Privacy Issues: Respect the privacy of individuals. When dealing with metadata, especially from social media, ensure that the analysis does not infringe upon personal privacy rights or local laws regarding data collection.

Accuracy of Data: Metadata can be manipulated or stripped away. Analysts should verify the authenticity of the metadata and consider the possibility of inaccuracies, particularly when relying on user-generated content.

Consent and Transparency: Whenever possible, obtain consent for using personal data, especially if the information will be shared or published. Transparency in the analysis process helps build trust and ensures ethical standards are maintained.

5. Practical Applications

Utilizing metadata for geolocation has practical applications in various fields, including:

Law Enforcement: Investigators can use metadata from crime scene photographs or social media posts to establish timelines and locations relevant to investigations.

Disaster Response: In emergency situations, analyzing metadata from social media can help responders locate people in distress and assess damage in real-time.

Market Research: Businesses can analyze location data from user-generated content to understand customer demographics and preferences based on geographic distribution.

Extracting and analyzing metadata from photos and posts provides a powerful method for determining geolocation in OSINT efforts. By leveraging tools for metadata extraction and employing analytical techniques to interpret the data, analysts can gain valuable insights into individuals' activities and movements. While this capability holds significant potential for intelligence gathering, ethical considerations surrounding privacy and data accuracy must be prioritized to ensure responsible usage. As technology advances, the methods for geolocation through metadata will continue to evolve, presenting new opportunities and challenges for OSINT practitioners.

4.2 Tools for Geo-Location: Overview of Google Earth, OpenStreetMap, and satellite imagery services.

Geo-location is an essential component of Open Source Intelligence (OSINT), providing analysts with critical insights into the geographical context of events, individuals, and data. Several powerful tools and platforms facilitate geo-location by offering detailed maps, satellite imagery, and community-driven geographic information. This section will provide an overview of three prominent geo-location tools: Google Earth, OpenStreetMap, and various satellite imagery services, exploring their features, applications, and benefits for OSINT practitioners.

1. Google Earth

Overview: Google Earth is a robust mapping application that provides users with a 3D representation of Earth, allowing for detailed exploration of geographical locations, landmarks, and terrain.

Key Features:

- **3D Visualization**: Google Earth offers a three-dimensional view of the Earth, enabling users to zoom in on specific locations and explore them from various angles. This feature enhances the understanding of geographical features and urban layouts.

- **Historical Imagery**: Users can access historical satellite imagery to compare changes in geographical areas over time. This capability is valuable for analyzing urban development, environmental changes, and disaster impact.
- **Street View**: Google Earth integrates Google Street View, allowing users to virtually explore streets and locations through panoramic photographs. This feature can help analysts visualize environments and context.

Use Cases:

- **Site Assessments**: Analysts can use Google Earth for site assessments, visualizing potential locations for events or operations. This tool can also aid in risk assessments for critical infrastructure.
- **Event Tracking**: During natural disasters or significant events, Google Earth can be used to monitor changes in the landscape, assess damage, and track relief efforts.
- **Benefits**: The interactive 3D visualization and extensive data make Google Earth a versatile tool for geo-location analysis, providing a comprehensive view of geographical contexts.

2. OpenStreetMap (OSM)

Overview: OpenStreetMap is a collaborative mapping platform that allows users to create and edit map data. It provides detailed, user-generated geographic information, making it a valuable resource for OSINT analysts.

Key Features:

- **Crowdsourced Data**: OpenStreetMap relies on contributions from volunteers worldwide, resulting in a rich and diverse dataset. Users can add features like roads, buildings, parks, and more, ensuring up-to-date geographic information.
- **Custom Map Creation**: Analysts can create custom maps using OSM data, highlighting specific features or areas of interest. This customization allows for tailored analyses based on specific needs.
- **Variety of Map Styles**: OSM offers various map styles, from standard maps to specialized versions (e.g., topographic, humanitarian) that cater to different analytical needs.

Use Cases:

- **Urban Planning**: City planners and local governments can use OpenStreetMap data to inform urban development projects and assess community needs based on geographical data.
- **Humanitarian Efforts**: During humanitarian crises, organizations can leverage OSM data to identify affected areas, plan relief efforts, and coordinate logistics efficiently.
- **Benefits**: The collaborative nature of OpenStreetMap fosters a sense of community while providing detailed and accurate geographic information, making it an indispensable tool for OSINT practitioners.

3. Satellite Imagery Services

Overview: Satellite imagery services provide high-resolution images of Earth's surface captured from space. These images are essential for monitoring geographical changes, analyzing landscapes, and conducting environmental assessments.

Key Features:

- **High-Resolution Images**: Satellite imagery services offer detailed images that can reveal small-scale features, such as buildings, vehicles, and land use patterns. This resolution allows for precise analysis of geographical areas.
- **Change Detection**: Many satellite services enable users to perform change detection analyses, comparing images taken at different times to identify alterations in the landscape due to urbanization, natural disasters, or environmental degradation.
- **Data Layers**: Some platforms provide additional data layers, such as vegetation indices, population density maps, and infrastructure data, enriching the analysis process.

Popular Services:

- **NASA's Earth Observing System Data and Information System (EOSDIS):** Offers access to a wide range of satellite imagery and data from NASA missions, focusing on environmental monitoring and climate change.
- **Google Earth Engine**: A cloud-based platform that allows users to analyze large datasets of satellite imagery for various applications, including environmental monitoring, disaster response, and agricultural assessments.
- **Planet Labs:** Provides daily satellite imagery of the entire Earth, allowing for real-time monitoring of changes and events. This service is especially useful for agricultural and environmental applications.

Use Cases:

- **Environmental Monitoring**: Satellite imagery is crucial for tracking deforestation, urbanization, and natural disasters, providing analysts with valuable insights into environmental changes.
- **Security and Defense**: Military and intelligence agencies use satellite imagery for reconnaissance, situational awareness, and monitoring geopolitical developments.
- **Benefits**: Satellite imagery services offer unparalleled insights into the Earth's surface, enabling detailed analysis and monitoring of geographical changes, making them invaluable for OSINT efforts.

Tools like Google Earth, OpenStreetMap, and satellite imagery services are essential for effective geo-location analysis in OSINT. Each tool offers unique features and capabilities that contribute to a comprehensive understanding of geographical contexts. By leveraging these resources, analysts can gather vital intelligence on individuals, events, and environments, enhancing their ability to make informed decisions. As technology continues to advance, the integration of geo-location tools into OSINT practices will play an increasingly critical role in data analysis and strategic planning across various fields.

4.3 Case Studies in Location Tracking: Real-world examples of using geolocation in OSINT investigations.

Geolocation in Open Source Intelligence (OSINT) plays a crucial role in a variety of investigations across fields such as law enforcement, journalism, disaster response, and security. By analyzing location data from digital sources, analysts can uncover significant insights that aid in understanding events, monitoring activities, and making informed decisions. This section presents real-world case studies showcasing how geolocation has been effectively utilized in OSINT investigations.

Case Study 1: Tracking Protests and Civil Unrest

Context: In recent years, global protests and civil unrest have become more visible through social media. Analysts and journalists have utilized geolocation tools to understand the dynamics of these events, assess crowd sizes, and monitor participant movement.

Example: The Black Lives Matter protests in the United States in 2020 serve as a prime example. Various OSINT practitioners analyzed posts from platforms like Twitter and Instagram, extracting metadata and geotagged information from images and videos shared by protesters.

Tools Used:

- **Social Media Analysis Tools**: Tools like TweetDeck and Social Searcher were employed to track specific hashtags (e.g., #BlackLivesMatter) and identify locations where protests were taking place.
- **Geolocation Software**: Analysts used Google Earth to visualize protest routes and hotspots by plotting geotagged posts on maps.
- **Outcomes**: The analysis allowed journalists and activists to identify key locations of unrest, monitor the scale of protests, and understand the evolution of demonstrations over time. This information was vital for both reporting and for local authorities in managing public safety.

Case Study 2: Environmental Monitoring and Illegal Logging

Context: Environmental NGOs and researchers have increasingly relied on geolocation data to monitor illegal activities that threaten ecosystems, such as illegal logging and poaching.

Example: A notable case occurred in the Amazon rainforest, where organizations used satellite imagery and open-source data to track deforestation activities.

Tools Used:

- **Satellite Imagery**: Platforms like NASA's Earth Observing System and Google Earth were employed to capture high-resolution images of the rainforest over time, allowing analysts to detect changes in land use.
- **OpenStreetMap**: Analysts used OSM to identify road networks and new clearings that correlated with illegal logging operations.
- **Outcomes**: The geolocation analysis provided compelling evidence of illegal logging activities, enabling NGOs to compile reports that prompted governmental and international action to protect the rainforest. This case demonstrated the effectiveness of OSINT in holding companies accountable for environmental violations.

Case Study 3: Investigating Cybercrime

Context: Law enforcement agencies worldwide increasingly use OSINT, including geolocation techniques, to combat cybercrime, such as human trafficking and online fraud.

Example: In a specific case, investigators sought to dismantle a human trafficking ring operating online. Analysts utilized geolocation data from social media profiles and website analytics to track the suspects' activities.

Tools Used:

- **Social Media Analysis**: Platforms like Facebook and Instagram were analyzed for geotagged images and posts that provided insights into the suspects' locations and networks.
- **Metadata Extraction Tools**: Tools like ExifTool were used to extract metadata from photos posted by suspects, revealing the GPS coordinates of their locations.
- **Outcomes**: By mapping the geolocation data collected from various digital sources, investigators could establish connections between suspects and specific locations, leading to coordinated raids and the rescue of trafficking victims. This case exemplifies the importance of geolocation in identifying and apprehending cybercriminals.

Case Study 4: Disaster Response and Recovery

Context: Following natural disasters, timely information is critical for response and recovery efforts. Geolocation tools help humanitarian organizations assess damage, coordinate relief efforts, and identify affected populations.

Example: After Hurricane Harvey struck Texas in 2017, various organizations utilized OSINT to manage disaster response effectively.

Tools Used:

- **Satellite Imagery**: High-resolution satellite images from services like Planet Labs were used to assess flood damage and identify infrastructure impacts.
- **Social Media Monitoring**: Organizations monitored Twitter and Facebook for geotagged posts and images from affected individuals, which provided real-time information about locations in need of assistance.
- **Outcomes**: The combination of satellite imagery and social media geolocation data enabled responders to allocate resources efficiently and prioritize areas

requiring immediate aid. The effective use of OSINT demonstrated the importance of geolocation in disaster management.

These case studies illustrate the diverse applications of geolocation in OSINT investigations, from monitoring protests and environmental changes to combating cybercrime and coordinating disaster response. By leveraging tools such as satellite imagery, social media analytics, and geolocation software, analysts can uncover critical insights that inform decision-making and actions across various fields. The ongoing advancements in geolocation technologies and methodologies will continue to enhance the effectiveness of OSINT, enabling practitioners to address complex challenges in an increasingly interconnected world.

Chapter 5: Analyzing Digital Footprints

Chapter 5, Analyzing Digital Footprints, delves into techniques for tracing and understanding an individual's online presence and behavior. This chapter guides readers through the process of compiling digital profiles by analyzing usernames, email addresses, IP addresses, and activity on various online platforms. Readers learn to uncover patterns, track behavioral clues, and connect pieces of information that reveal a more complete picture of an individual or entity. The chapter also covers strategies to minimize one's own digital footprint, offering practical advice on digital privacy and security. By the end, readers will be equipped to both trace digital histories effectively and protect themselves in the digital sphere.

5.1 Digital Profile Building: Compiling profiles from usernames, email addresses, and other online identifiers.

In the realm of Open Source Intelligence (OSINT), digital profile building is a fundamental practice that involves gathering and synthesizing information from various online identifiers to create comprehensive profiles of individuals. These profiles can provide insights into a person's online behavior, interests, connections, and even potential vulnerabilities. This section will explore the methods and tools for compiling profiles using usernames, email addresses, and other digital identifiers, highlighting the importance of ethical considerations throughout the process.

1. Understanding Digital Profiles

A digital profile is a compilation of information collected from various online sources that reflect an individual's online presence. These profiles can include:

- **Usernames**: Unique identifiers that people use across different platforms, which can reveal their interests or affiliations.
- **Email Addresses**: Often linked to various accounts and can provide insights into an individual's activities and subscriptions.
- **Social Media Accounts**: Platforms like Facebook, Twitter, Instagram, and LinkedIn, where individuals share personal information and interact with others.
- **Public Records**: Information available from government databases or public forums that may relate to an individual's history or activities.

2. Methods for Profile Building

To effectively compile a digital profile, OSINT practitioners employ various methods and tools. Here's a structured approach to building digital profiles using online identifiers:

2.1 Collecting Usernames

Usernames can serve as the starting point for profile building. Here's how to gather and analyze usernames:

- **Search Engines**: Start with a search engine query using the username in quotation marks (e.g., "exampleUsername"). This can reveal accounts on different platforms, public forums, or blogs.
- **Social Media Search**: Many social media platforms have search functions that allow users to search for usernames directly. Utilizing platforms like Twitter, Instagram, and Reddit can uncover associated accounts.
- **Username Checkers**: Tools like KnowEm or Namechk can help verify the availability of a username across multiple platforms, indicating where a person may have an account.

2.2 Analyzing Email Addresses

Email addresses can be rich sources of information when building a digital profile:

- **Email Lookup Services**: Tools like Hunter.io or VoilaNorbert allow users to input email addresses and retrieve associated names, social profiles, and more. This can help identify the individual behind an email address.
- **Data Breach Sites**: Websites like Have I Been Pwned provide information on whether an email address has been part of any data breaches, indicating the potential for compromised information.
- **Social Media Connections**: Inputting an email address into platforms like LinkedIn can sometimes reveal associated accounts, as many users link their email addresses to their profiles.

2.3 Gathering Information from Social Media

Social media platforms are treasure troves of information. Here's how to compile data from them:

- **Profile Scraping**: Tools like PhantomBuster or Social Searcher can be used to scrape public data from social media profiles based on usernames or email addresses.
- **Content Analysis**: Analyzing the content shared by individuals, such as posts, likes, and comments, can provide insights into their interests, affiliations, and social circles.
- **Connection Mapping**: Mapping out connections and interactions between individuals on social media can help identify relationships and networks, revealing more about a person's social landscape.

2.4 Exploring Public Records

Public records can provide additional context for a digital profile:

- **Government Databases**: Accessing public records databases can yield information on property ownership, legal filings, and more. Websites like Whitepages or Spokeo can help locate this information.
- **Professional Licenses**: Certain professions require licensing, and databases that track licenses can provide insights into a person's career and qualifications.
- **Voter Registration and Criminal Records**: Public access to voter registration and criminal records can shed light on a person's history, although availability may vary by jurisdiction.

3. Tools for Digital Profile Building

Several tools can assist in the process of digital profile building, enhancing efficiency and effectiveness:

- **Maltego**: A powerful data mining tool that allows users to visualize relationships between various digital entities, including usernames and email addresses.
- **OSINT Framework**: A collection of tools and resources organized by data types that can aid in various aspects of OSINT investigations, including digital profile building.
- **SpiderFoot**: An open-source tool that automates the collection of OSINT data from a wide range of sources, helping to build comprehensive profiles based on usernames or email addresses.

4. Ethical Considerations

While digital profile building can be an effective investigative technique, ethical considerations are paramount:

- **Privacy Rights**: Respect individuals' privacy rights and be aware of local laws regarding data collection and privacy. Gathering information without consent can lead to ethical and legal ramifications.
- **Data Accuracy**: Be cautious of the accuracy of the data collected. Cross-verify information from multiple sources to avoid relying on inaccurate or misleading information.
- **Responsible Use**: Ensure that the compiled profiles are used responsibly, with a focus on legitimate purposes such as research, security assessments, or law enforcement.

Digital profile building through usernames, email addresses, and other online identifiers is a critical practice in OSINT investigations. By employing various methods and tools, analysts can compile comprehensive profiles that provide valuable insights into individuals' online behaviors and networks. However, it is essential to navigate the ethical landscape carefully, respecting privacy rights and ensuring responsible use of the information gathered. As the digital landscape continues to evolve, the techniques for building digital profiles will also adapt, offering new opportunities and challenges for OSINT practitioners.

5.2 Techniques to Trace Digital Behavior: Methods for tracking an individual's online habits, interests, and routines.

Tracing an individual's digital behavior involves systematically collecting and analyzing data from various online activities to understand their habits, interests, and routines. In the realm of Open Source Intelligence (OSINT), this practice can be invaluable for various applications, including cybersecurity, criminal investigations, and market research. This section explores effective techniques for tracking digital behavior, highlighting the tools and methods used to gather and analyze this information.

1. Understanding Digital Behavior

Digital behavior refers to the actions and patterns displayed by individuals while interacting with online platforms. This can include:

- **Browsing History**: Websites visited, frequency of visits, and duration of engagement.
- **Social Media Activity**: Posts, likes, shares, comments, and interactions with others.
- **Search Queries**: Search terms used on platforms like Google, which can reveal interests and priorities.
- **Purchase Patterns**: Transactions made on e-commerce sites and subscriptions to services or newsletters.

Understanding these behaviors provides insights into an individual's preferences, routines, and potential vulnerabilities.

2. Techniques for Tracking Digital Behavior

2.1 Analyzing Social Media Activity

Social media platforms are rich sources of data regarding an individual's interests and habits. Analysts can employ several techniques to trace digital behavior on these platforms:

Content Analysis:

- **Posts and Comments**: Reviewing the content shared by an individual (text, images, videos) can reveal interests, affiliations, and sentiments. This analysis can be done manually or through text analysis tools to identify themes and topics.
- **Engagement Metrics**: Analyzing likes, shares, and comments can provide insights into the types of content that resonate with the individual. Tools like BuzzSumo can help identify popular content within specific topics.

Network Analysis:

- **Connection Mapping**: Using tools like Maltego or Gephi, analysts can visualize relationships between users based on interactions, helping to identify influential connections and social circles.
- **Follower/Following Patterns**: Analyzing the individuals an account follows and is followed by can provide insights into their interests and affiliations.

2.2 Monitoring Online Behavior with Browser Fingerprinting

Browser fingerprinting is a technique that collects various attributes from a user's browser to create a unique identifier. This can help track an individual's online behavior across websites.

Attributes Collected: Browser fingerprinting can collect information such as:

- Browser type and version
- Operating system
- Installed plugins and fonts
- Screen resolution and color depth

Use Cases:

- **Behavioral Analysis**: Companies often use fingerprinting to understand user behavior across websites for marketing and product development purposes. In OSINT, this technique can help identify recurring patterns in an individual's online activities.
- **Tools**: Tools like FingerprintJS can help developers implement browser fingerprinting techniques to track user behavior.

2.3 Examining Search Behavior

Search behavior can provide significant insights into an individual's interests, concerns, and information-seeking patterns.

Google Search Queries:

Analysts can use tools like Google Trends to explore search trends related to specific keywords over time. This can reveal interests and concerns based on popular search terms.

Analyzing query auto-suggestions and "People also ask" sections can help understand what topics an individual may be researching.

SEO Tools: Tools like Ahrefs and SEMrush can provide insights into the search queries that drive traffic to specific websites, allowing analysts to infer an individual's interests based on their browsing history.

2.4 Tracking E-Commerce Behavior

E-commerce platforms provide data that can be analyzed to understand an individual's purchasing habits and interests.

Purchase History Analysis:

If accessible, reviewing an individual's transaction history (e.g., via receipts, order confirmations) can reveal buying patterns, preferred brands, and even lifestyle choices.

Analysts can use web scraping tools (e.g., Beautiful Soup or Scrapy) to extract publicly available e-commerce data for analysis.

Subscription Services: Many individuals subscribe to services like streaming platforms, newsletters, or shopping services. Analyzing these subscriptions can provide insights into interests and routines.

2.5 Leveraging Digital Footprints

A digital footprint refers to the trail of data individuals leave behind while using the internet. This includes data from social media, websites visited, and online transactions. Techniques to analyze digital footprints include:

- **Public Records**: Many public records are available online and can provide additional context about an individual's activities and affiliations.
- **Geo-Location Data**: Combining location data from social media check-ins, geotagged photos, and GPS information can help trace an individual's routines and frequent locations.
- **Online Forums and Communities**: Participation in online forums or discussion groups can reveal interests and opinions. Analysts can track usernames across multiple platforms to gather comprehensive data.

3. Tools for Tracking Digital Behavior

Several tools can assist analysts in tracing digital behavior:

Social Media Monitoring Tools:

- Hootsuite and Buffer allow for tracking social media interactions, engagements, and content performance.
- Brandwatch and Mention help in monitoring online mentions and sentiment analysis related to specific topics or individuals.

Web Analytics Tools:

- Google Analytics provides insights into website traffic and user behavior, allowing analysts to infer interests based on browsing patterns.
- Hotjar offers heatmaps and session recordings that show how users interact with a website.

Data Mining Tools:

- Tools like Octoparse and Import.io facilitate web scraping and data extraction from various online sources, enabling analysts to gather and analyze data efficiently.

4. Ethical Considerations

Tracking digital behavior raises important ethical considerations:

- **Privacy Concerns**: Analysts must respect individuals' privacy rights and comply with relevant data protection regulations (e.g., GDPR, CCPA) when collecting and analyzing data.
- **Data Accuracy**: It's crucial to ensure that the data collected is accurate and reliable, as misinterpretation can lead to erroneous conclusions.
- **Responsible Use**: Information gathered should be used responsibly, with a focus on legitimate purposes, such as security assessments, research, or investigative efforts.

Tracing digital behavior through techniques such as analyzing social media activity, monitoring online behavior, examining search patterns, and leveraging digital footprints is a vital aspect of OSINT. By employing these methods and utilizing various tools, analysts can gain comprehensive insights into an individual's online habits, interests, and routines. However, it is essential to navigate the ethical landscape carefully, ensuring privacy rights are respected and that data is used responsibly. As technology evolves, so too will the techniques for tracking digital behavior, providing new opportunities and challenges for OSINT practitioners.

5.3 Protecting Your Own Digital Footprint: Practical strategies to minimize personal exposure online.

In an increasingly connected world, our digital footprints— the trails of data we leave behind as we navigate the internet— are more visible than ever. This footprint encompasses everything from social media posts and online purchases to browsing histories and geolocation data. Understanding how to manage and protect your digital footprint is crucial for safeguarding your personal information and maintaining privacy. This section outlines practical strategies for minimizing personal exposure online, helping individuals take control of their digital identities.

1. Understanding Your Digital Footprint

A digital footprint consists of two main types:

- **Active Footprint**: This is the data you intentionally share online, such as social media posts, blog entries, and online reviews.
- **Passive Footprint**: This refers to data collected without your explicit input, including browsing habits, cookies, location data, and metadata from your online activities.

Recognizing the extent of your digital footprint is the first step in managing it effectively.

2. Practical Strategies for Minimizing Your Digital Footprint

2.1 Review and Adjust Privacy Settings

Most online platforms offer privacy settings that allow users to control who can see their information. To minimize exposure:

- **Social Media**: Regularly review privacy settings on platforms like Facebook, Instagram, and Twitter. Adjust settings to limit visibility to friends only, and be cautious about accepting friend requests from unknown individuals.
- **Profile Information**: Limit the personal information you share in your profiles. Avoid providing sensitive details like your phone number, address, or date of birth.
- **Geolocation Settings**: Turn off location services for apps unless necessary. For social media, avoid geotagging posts and check-ins.

2.2 Use Strong Passwords and Two-Factor Authentication (2FA)

Strong passwords are a fundamental component of online security. Implement the following practices:

- **Complex Passwords**: Use unique passwords for different accounts, incorporating letters, numbers, and symbols. Aim for a minimum length of 12 characters.
- **Password Managers**: Consider using a password manager to store and generate strong passwords securely. Tools like LastPass, 1Password, or Dashlane can simplify password management.
- **Two-Factor Authentication (2FA):** Enable 2FA on all accounts that offer it. This adds an extra layer of security by requiring a secondary verification method, such as a code sent to your phone.

2.3 Limit Sharing of Personal Information

Being mindful of the information you share online can significantly reduce your digital footprint:

- **Think Before You Share**: Consider the implications of sharing personal stories or photos online. Even seemingly harmless information can be pieced together to form a larger picture of your identity.
- **Be Cautious with Online Forms**: Only provide necessary information when filling out forms, whether for subscriptions, contests, or online purchases. Opt out of non-essential fields whenever possible.
- **Anonymous Browsing**: Use tools like Tor or privacy-focused browsers like Brave to browse the internet anonymously, minimizing the data collected during your online activities.

2.4 Regularly Audit Your Digital Presence

Performing a regular audit of your online presence can help you identify and manage unwanted exposure:

- **Google Yourself**: Conduct searches using your name and related identifiers (like email addresses) to see what information is publicly accessible. This can help you identify outdated or unwanted content.
- **Delete Old Accounts**: If you have unused accounts on platforms or services, consider deleting them. Many services, like JustDeleteMe, can help you find links to delete your accounts easily.
- **Manage Your Online Reputation**: Use reputation management tools like BrandYourself to help monitor and manage your online presence. These tools can alert you to new mentions of your name or personal information.

2.5 Be Cautious with Public Wi-Fi

Public Wi-Fi networks can expose users to significant security risks. To protect your data:

- **Avoid Sensitive Transactions**: Do not conduct sensitive transactions, like online banking or shopping, while connected to public Wi-Fi.
- **Use a Virtual Private Network (VPN):** A VPN encrypts your internet connection, making it harder for third parties to intercept your data. Services like NordVPN, ExpressVPN, or CyberGhost can provide added security on public networks.

2.6 Understand Data Collection and Online Tracking

Being aware of how websites and apps collect data can help you make informed decisions:

- **Browser Privacy Settings**: Adjust your browser settings to block third-party cookies and trackers. Most modern browsers have built-in options to enhance privacy.
- **Use Privacy Extensions**: Tools like uBlock Origin, Privacy Badger, or Ghostery can help block ads and trackers, limiting the data collected during your browsing sessions.

2.7 Educate Yourself About Phishing and Scams

Cybercriminals often use social engineering tactics to gather personal information. To protect yourself:

- **Recognize Phishing Attempts**: Be wary of unsolicited emails, messages, or phone calls asking for personal information. Verify the sender's identity before responding.
- **Avoid Clicking Unknown Links**: Do not click on links or download attachments from unknown sources, as they may lead to malware or data breaches.

Protecting your digital footprint is essential in today's interconnected world. By implementing practical strategies—such as reviewing privacy settings, using strong passwords, limiting personal information sharing, and regularly auditing your digital presence—individuals can minimize their exposure online and enhance their privacy. Staying informed about online security threats and data collection practices is also crucial in safeguarding personal information. By taking proactive steps, you can effectively manage your digital footprint and maintain control over your online identity.

Chapter 6: Investigating Domains, Websites, and IPs

Chapter 6, Investigating Domains, Websites, and IPs, focuses on techniques for uncovering vital information related to internet domains, websites, and their associated IP addresses. This chapter introduces readers to WHOIS databases and DNS records, explaining how to access and interpret this information to gain insights into domain ownership and history. Readers will learn how to perform reverse IP lookups to identify other domains hosted on the same server and understand the implications of web hosting details. The chapter emphasizes the importance of analyzing website content and structure, including metadata and updates, to detect potential malicious activities or threats. Through practical examples, readers will develop the skills necessary to navigate and extract intelligence from the digital landscape of domains and websites, enhancing their investigative capabilities.

6.1 Using WHOIS and DNS Records: How to leverage domain registration and DNS data for OSINT.

In the realm of Open Source Intelligence (OSINT), understanding domain registration and DNS (Domain Name System) records can provide crucial insights into the ownership, management, and infrastructure of websites. WHOIS data offers details about who registered a domain, while DNS records contain information about how that domain functions on the internet. This section explores how to effectively leverage WHOIS and DNS data for investigative purposes.

1. Understanding WHOIS Data

WHOIS is a query and response protocol used to obtain information about registered domain names and IP addresses. When someone registers a domain name, they must provide certain details, which are stored in a WHOIS database. The information available typically includes:

- **Domain Registrant Information**: The name, organization, and contact details of the individual or entity that registered the domain.
- **Registration Dates**: The date the domain was created, the date it was last updated, and the expiration date.

- **Registrar Information**: The company responsible for managing the domain registration.
- **Name Server Information**: The DNS servers that manage the domain's DNS records.

WHOIS data can be valuable in various OSINT applications, including cybersecurity investigations, competitive analysis, and identifying potential threats.

2. How to Access WHOIS Information

There are multiple ways to access WHOIS data:

- **WHOIS Lookup Tools**: Websites like whois.domaintools.com, whois.net, and ICANN WHOIS allow users to input a domain name and retrieve its registration details.
- **Command Line Tools**: For those comfortable with the command line, the whois command can be run directly in Linux and macOS terminals. For example:

whois example.com

3. Leveraging WHOIS Data for OSINT

Once you have access to WHOIS data, there are several ways to leverage this information for investigative purposes:

3.1 Identifying Domain Ownership

Understanding who owns a domain can be pivotal in investigations. For instance:

- **Investigating Malicious Domains**: If a domain is linked to phishing or cybercrime, WHOIS data can help identify the registrant, potentially leading to actionable intelligence about their identity or related domains.
- **Competitor Research**: Businesses can analyze their competitors' domain registrations to identify their online strategies, such as new product launches or services.

3.2 Tracking Domain Changes

WHOIS records often contain information about when a domain was registered and updated:

- **Monitoring Changes**: By regularly checking WHOIS data, analysts can track changes in domain ownership or registration details, which may signal suspicious activity.
- **Expiration and Renewal Patterns**: Observing when domains expire or are renewed can provide insights into an organization's operational status or intent.

3.3 Mapping Relationships Between Domains

WHOIS data can help analysts understand relationships between different domains:

- **Identifying Related Domains**: If multiple domains are registered to the same individual or organization, this information can help uncover potential connections in cyber activities or business practices.
- **Domain Squatting**: Analysts can identify potential domain squatters who register similar domain names to exploit the reputation of established brands.

4. Understanding DNS Records

DNS records provide critical information about how a domain functions on the internet. Key types of DNS records include:

- **A Record**: Maps a domain name to an IP address, allowing users to find the website.
- **MX Record**: Specifies the mail servers responsible for receiving email for the domain.
- **CNAME Record**: Allows one domain to be an alias for another, directing users to the target domain's IP address.
- **NS Record**: Indicates the name servers responsible for managing the DNS records of a domain.
- **TXT Record**: Can contain various types of text information, including verification for domain ownership or security policies.

5. Accessing DNS Records

DNS records can be accessed through various methods:

- **DNS Lookup Tools**: Online tools like MXToolbox, DNSstuff, and ViewDNS.info allow users to query DNS records for any domain.

- **Command Line Tools**: The dig command in Unix-based systems is a powerful way to query DNS records. For example:

dig example.com ANY

6. Leveraging DNS Data for OSINT

DNS data can be extremely useful for OSINT investigations. Here are ways to utilize it:

6.1 Identifying Hosting Providers

By examining A records, analysts can determine the IP addresses associated with a domain. This can help:

Identify Hosting Providers: Understanding where a website is hosted can provide insights into its operational security and reliability. If a domain is hosted on a known provider associated with malicious activity, this could be a red flag.

6.2 Analyzing Email Infrastructure

MX records can provide insights into the email systems used by an organization:

Assessing Security Posture: Knowing which email providers a domain uses can help assess its security measures. For instance, if a domain uses free email services without additional security protocols, it may be more vulnerable to attacks.

6.3 Tracing Connections

By examining CNAME records, analysts can identify relationships between domains and services:

Mapping Dependencies: Analyzing CNAME records can reveal if a domain relies on third-party services or subdomains, providing insights into its operational structure and dependencies.

7. Ethical Considerations

When leveraging WHOIS and DNS data, it's essential to remain mindful of ethical considerations:

Respecting Privacy: Many domain registrars offer privacy protection services to keep registrant information confidential. Analysts should respect these privacy measures and focus on publicly available information.

Legitimate Use: Ensure that any data gathered is used for ethical purposes, such as cybersecurity, research, or legitimate business analysis.

WHOIS and DNS records are invaluable resources in the OSINT toolkit. By understanding how to access and analyze this data, investigators can uncover vital insights about domain ownership, relationships, and online infrastructure. These insights can be applied in various contexts, from cybersecurity investigations to competitive analysis. However, it's crucial to approach this information ethically and responsibly, ensuring that the data is used for legitimate purposes. As the digital landscape continues to evolve, leveraging WHOIS and DNS data will remain a critical aspect of effective OSINT practices.

6.2 Reverse IP and Hosting Analysis: Techniques to uncover connections between IPs, hosts, and domains.

In the realm of Open Source Intelligence (OSINT), understanding the connections between IP addresses, hosting providers, and domains is essential for revealing relationships and uncovering potentially malicious activities. Reverse IP and hosting analysis can provide critical insights that contribute to a more comprehensive understanding of online entities, aiding in investigations ranging from cybersecurity to competitive analysis. This section explores techniques to leverage reverse IP and hosting analysis effectively.

1. Understanding Reverse IP Lookup

Reverse IP lookup is a method used to identify all domain names associated with a specific IP address. This technique allows investigators to see which websites share the same server and can indicate relationships between seemingly unrelated domains.

1.1 Importance of Reverse IP Lookup

- **Identifying Shared Hosting**: Many websites are hosted on shared servers, meaning multiple domains reside on the same IP address. Analyzing these connections can help identify relationships and potential associations among different entities.

- **Detecting Malicious Activities**: If a known malicious domain shares an IP address with another domain, it may raise red flags regarding the integrity of the latter, suggesting potential involvement in cybercriminal activities.

2. Tools for Reverse IP Lookup

Several tools and services facilitate reverse IP lookups, providing investigators with valuable data:

- **DomainTools**: This service allows users to perform reverse IP lookups and view associated domains. It also offers historical data to identify changes over time.
- **ViewDNS**: A versatile tool that provides a reverse IP lookup feature, along with DNS information and other useful data about domains.
- **Spyse**: This cybersecurity search engine offers extensive information about IP addresses, including the ability to find all domains hosted on a specific IP.

Example of a Reverse IP Lookup

To perform a reverse IP lookup using a tool like ViewDNS:

- Navigate to the reverse IP lookup section.
- Enter the IP address you wish to analyze.

Review the list of domains associated with that IP, which may reveal connections or related entities.

3. Understanding Hosting Analysis

Hosting analysis involves investigating the characteristics of the server that hosts a domain. This includes identifying the hosting provider, examining server configurations, and assessing the security posture of the hosting environment.

3.1 Importance of Hosting Analysis

- **Identifying Hosting Providers**: Knowing who hosts a domain can provide insights into its reliability and security. Some hosting providers are associated with high levels of malicious activity, while others are known for robust security measures.
- **Assessing Server Environment**: Analyzing server configurations can reveal vulnerabilities that may expose hosted websites to security threats.

4. Techniques for Hosting Analysis

4.1 WHOIS Lookup

As discussed in the previous section, WHOIS lookups provide essential information about domain registration, including hosting details:

- **Registrar Information**: The registrar often offers insight into the hosting provider, especially if the domain is registered with a web hosting service.
- **Name Server Information**: Analyzing name servers can indicate which provider manages the DNS records, often correlating with the hosting provider.

4.2 DNS Record Analysis

Examining DNS records provides valuable information about the domain's hosting:

- **A Records**: These records map domain names to IP addresses, allowing analysts to identify the hosting server.
- **MX Records**: Analyzing mail server information can provide additional context about the domain's operations, especially if it uses a specific hosting provider for email services.

4.3 Using Online Tools

Several online tools can assist in hosting analysis:

- **IPinfo**: Provides detailed information about an IP address, including the hosting provider, geographical location, and other related domains.
- **WhoisXML API**: Offers various APIs that allow for extensive querying of domain and IP data, facilitating deeper analysis of hosting environments and domain associations.

5. Case Studies and Applications

5.1 Cybersecurity Investigations

In cybersecurity investigations, reverse IP and hosting analysis can help identify potential threats:

- **Identifying Phishing Campaigns**: If a known phishing domain shares an IP address with a legitimate organization, it may indicate a targeted attack or exploitation of brand reputation.
- **Uncovering Malicious Infrastructure**: Investigators can reveal networks of malicious domains that share hosting resources, allowing for the dismantling of cybercriminal operations.

5.2 Competitive Analysis

In competitive analysis, understanding the hosting environment can yield valuable insights:

- **Identifying Market Strategies**: Businesses can monitor competitors' hosting arrangements to identify potential partnerships, acquisitions, or shifts in strategy.
- **Evaluating Security Posture**: Analyzing the hosting security of competitors can provide insights into their vulnerability to attacks, helping to inform strategic decisions.

6. Ethical Considerations

When conducting reverse IP and hosting analysis, it is essential to adhere to ethical standards:

- **Respect Privacy**: Always respect the privacy of individuals and organizations. Use the gathered information responsibly and avoid malicious intent.
- **Legitimate Use**: Ensure that your investigations serve a legitimate purpose, whether in cybersecurity, market analysis, or academic research.

Reverse IP and hosting analysis are powerful techniques in the OSINT arsenal, allowing investigators to uncover connections between IPs, hosts, and domains. By leveraging these techniques, analysts can gain valuable insights into relationships, identify potential threats, and assess the security posture of online entities. With the right tools and methodologies, reverse IP and hosting analysis can significantly enhance the effectiveness of OSINT investigations, contributing to a deeper understanding of the digital landscape. However, it is crucial to conduct these analyses ethically and responsibly, ensuring that the information gathered is used for legitimate purposes.

6.3 Investigating Website Content: How to analyze website structure, metadata, and content updates.

In the field of Open Source Intelligence (OSINT), investigating website content is a critical aspect of understanding an organization's online presence, uncovering potential threats, and gathering intelligence about its operations. By analyzing the structure, metadata, and content updates of a website, investigators can derive valuable insights that can assist in various investigative scenarios, from cybersecurity assessments to competitive analysis. This section outlines techniques for effectively analyzing website content and what information can be gleaned from it.

1. Understanding Website Structure

The structure of a website encompasses its layout, design, and organization of content. A well-structured website not only enhances user experience but also provides insights into the organization's priorities and areas of focus.

1.1 Key Components of Website Structure

- **Navigation and Menus**: The main navigation menus and sub-menus reveal how information is categorized and prioritized. Observing the hierarchy can indicate the importance of various sections.
- **URL Structure**: Analyzing the URLs can provide insights into the organization's content strategy. Clean, descriptive URLs often reflect a well-thought-out site architecture.
- **Sitemaps**: Many websites have an XML sitemap that lists all the pages on the site. This can be accessed by appending /sitemap.xml to the website's URL (e.g., example.com/sitemap.xml). Sitemaps can reveal hidden pages or sections not easily accessible from the main navigation.

2. Tools for Analyzing Website Structure

Several tools can aid in analyzing the structure of a website:

- **Screaming Frog SEO Spider**: This tool allows users to crawl websites and collect data about structure, metadata, and content. It provides insights into the number of pages, URL structure, and potential issues.
- **Google Search Console**: This tool provides insights into how Google views a website, including indexed pages, crawl errors, and performance metrics.

- **Ahrefs and SEMrush**: These tools offer extensive site audit features that can analyze website structure, backlinks, and performance, giving a comprehensive view of a site's online presence.

3. Analyzing Metadata

Metadata refers to data that describes other data and provides essential context about the content on a website. It can include information about the page title, descriptions, keywords, and authorship.

3.1 Types of Metadata

- **Title Tags**: The title tag appears in search engine results and provides a brief summary of the page's content. Analyzing title tags can reveal how organizations position themselves and optimize for search engines.
- **Meta Descriptions**: These are short descriptions that summarize the content of the page. They play a crucial role in SEO and can provide insights into the key themes the organization wants to communicate.
- **Header Tags**: HTML header tags (H1, H2, H3) are used to structure content hierarchically. Analyzing these tags can reveal the main topics and subtopics covered on a page.

3.2 Accessing Metadata

Website metadata can be accessed using various methods:

- **Browser Developer Tools**: Most modern browsers allow users to inspect the source code of a webpage. By right-clicking on a page and selecting "Inspect," users can view the HTML structure, including metadata within the <head> section.
- **SEO Analysis Tools**: Tools like Moz, Ahrefs, and SEMrush provide metadata analysis features that can summarize key metadata for each page on a website.

4. Tracking Content Updates

Monitoring content updates on a website can reveal changes in organizational focus, new initiatives, or responses to current events. Tracking these changes is crucial for understanding trends and potential impacts on stakeholders.

4.1 Techniques for Tracking Updates

- **Change Detection Tools**: Services like Visualping or Wachete can notify users when changes are made to specific webpages. These tools can track updates to content, layout, or metadata.
- **Web Archives**: Using services like Wayback Machine allows users to view historical snapshots of a website. This can be valuable for understanding how a website has evolved over time, including changes in messaging or focus.
- **RSS Feeds**: Many websites provide RSS feeds that deliver updates whenever new content is published. Subscribing to these feeds can help keep track of new articles, blog posts, or announcements.

4.2 Analyzing Update Patterns

- **Frequency of Updates**: Tracking how often a website updates its content can provide insights into its operational priorities. Frequent updates may indicate an active engagement with current trends or a responsive marketing strategy.
- **Types of Content Updated**: Analyzing what types of content are regularly updated (e.g., blogs, news articles, product pages) can indicate the organization's focus areas and target audience.

5. Ethical Considerations

When investigating website content, it is essential to remain aware of ethical considerations:

- **Respect Privacy**: Be cautious not to invade the privacy of individuals or organizations. Use publicly available information responsibly and avoid malicious intent.
- **Legitimate Use**: Ensure that any data gathered is used for legitimate purposes, such as cybersecurity, competitive analysis, or academic research.

Investigating website content is a vital aspect of OSINT, providing insights into an organization's structure, focus areas, and operational dynamics. By analyzing website structure, metadata, and content updates, investigators can uncover valuable information that informs decision-making and enhances understanding of the digital landscape. Utilizing the right tools and methodologies allows for a thorough examination of websites, revealing connections and trends that may not be immediately apparent. However, ethical considerations should always be prioritized, ensuring that investigations are conducted responsibly and for legitimate purposes.

Chapter 7: OSINT and Cybercrime Investigation

Chapter 7, OSINT and Cybercrime Investigation, explores the critical role of open-source intelligence in identifying, tracking, and mitigating cybercriminal activities. This chapter outlines various types of cybercrime, including phishing, identity theft, and hacking, and discusses how OSINT techniques can be leveraged to uncover patterns and gather evidence. Readers will learn about specific tools and methodologies for monitoring online forums, social media, and the dark web to track criminal behavior and gather actionable intelligence. The chapter includes real-world case studies that illustrate successful OSINT applications in cybercrime investigations, demonstrating how investigators can connect the dots and piece together digital evidence. By the end of this chapter, readers will be equipped with practical skills and insights to effectively utilize OSINT in combating cyber threats and enhancing their overall cybersecurity efforts.

7.1 Identifying Cybercrime Patterns: Common patterns and indicators of cybercriminal behavior.

As the digital landscape continues to evolve, so too does the complexity and frequency of cybercrime. Identifying patterns and indicators of cybercriminal behavior is crucial for effective investigation, prevention, and response strategies. This section explores common patterns of cybercrime, the behaviors exhibited by cybercriminals, and how investigators can leverage this information to anticipate and mitigate cyber threats.

1. Understanding Cybercrime Patterns

Cybercrime patterns are recurring behaviors or actions exhibited by cybercriminals when they commit crimes online. By analyzing these patterns, investigators can gain insights into the methodologies used by criminals, which can aid in both prevention and detection.

1.1 Types of Cybercrime

Cybercrime can be broadly categorized into several types, including:

- **Hacking**: Unauthorized access to systems or networks to steal or manipulate data.
- **Phishing**: Fraudulent attempts to obtain sensitive information by disguising as a trustworthy entity.

- **Ransomware**: Malicious software that encrypts a victim's data, demanding payment for decryption.
- **Identity Theft**: Illegally obtaining and using someone else's personal information for fraudulent purposes.
- **Online Fraud**: Various schemes that exploit internet platforms to deceive individuals or businesses for financial gain.

2. Common Patterns of Cybercriminal Behavior

Understanding common patterns in cybercriminal behavior can help investigators and organizations develop strategies to counteract cybercrime effectively. Here are some key indicators:

2.1 Repeated Targeting of Specific Sectors

Cybercriminals often focus on specific sectors that may have weaker security measures or hold valuable data:

- **Healthcare**: With sensitive patient information and financial data, healthcare organizations are prime targets for ransomware attacks.
- **Financial Services**: Banks and payment processors are frequently targeted for phishing and fraud due to the potential for significant financial gain.
- **Retail**: E-commerce sites are often attacked for credit card information and personal data.

2.2 Geographical Concentration

Certain geographical areas are more prone to specific types of cybercrime, often influenced by regional economic factors, technology adoption, and law enforcement resources:

- **High-Income Areas**: Cybercriminals may target high-income regions due to the likelihood of finding wealthy individuals or businesses with valuable data.
- **Countries with Weak Cyber Laws**: Regions with less stringent cybersecurity regulations can become hotspots for cybercriminal activities, as perpetrators may operate with reduced fear of legal repercussions.

2.3 Use of Common Tools and Techniques

Cybercriminals often employ similar tools and techniques across various attacks, making these identifiable patterns:

- **Malware**: The use of specific malware types, such as ransomware or keyloggers, can be a strong indicator of cybercriminal intent.
- **Social Engineering**: Cybercriminals frequently utilize social engineering tactics, such as impersonating trusted individuals or organizations, to manipulate victims into divulging sensitive information.

3. Indicators of Cybercriminal Activity

Identifying potential indicators of cybercriminal behavior can help organizations and investigators respond proactively to threats. Some common indicators include:

3.1 Unusual Network Activity

Monitoring network activity can reveal abnormal patterns that may indicate cybercriminal behavior:

- **Excessive Login Attempts**: A high number of failed login attempts from a specific IP address can signal a brute-force attack.
- **Data Exfiltration**: Unusual outbound traffic volumes or unauthorized access to sensitive files may indicate data theft in progress.

3.2 Anomalous User Behavior

Changes in user behavior can signal potential cyber threats:

- **Account Compromise**: If a user account starts exhibiting unusual activity, such as accessing data outside of normal working hours or from unfamiliar locations, it could indicate a compromise.
- **Unauthorized Software Installation**: The installation of unknown applications on systems can indicate potential malware infiltration or malicious intent.

3.3 Communication Patterns

Analyzing communication patterns can provide insights into cybercriminal networks:

- **Frequent Communication with Known Malicious Domains**: Increased communication with domains associated with known cybercriminal activities can suggest involvement in malicious operations.
- **Use of Encrypted Communication Channels**: Cybercriminals may use encrypted messaging platforms or VPNs to communicate securely, making detection more challenging.

4. Leveraging Cybercrime Patterns for Investigation

Investigators can utilize identified patterns and indicators to enhance their OSINT efforts:

4.1 Threat Intelligence Sharing

Collaborating with other organizations to share threat intelligence can help identify patterns across different sectors and regions, allowing for a more comprehensive understanding of emerging threats.

- **Participating in Information Sharing Groups**: Many sectors have established information-sharing frameworks where organizations can report incidents and share threat data.
- **Utilizing Threat Intelligence Platforms**: Tools that aggregate and analyze threat intelligence data can help organizations identify patterns and trends in cybercriminal behavior.

4.2 Proactive Monitoring

Continuous monitoring of network activity, user behavior, and communication patterns can help detect potential threats early.

- **Implementing Security Information and Event Management (SIEM)**: SIEM solutions can aggregate data from multiple sources, enabling real-time analysis and alerts for anomalous activities.
- **Conducting Regular Security Audits**: Regular audits of systems and networks can help identify vulnerabilities and potential indicators of compromise.

Identifying patterns and indicators of cybercriminal behavior is essential for effective OSINT and cybersecurity strategies. By understanding common cybercrime patterns and the typical behaviors exhibited by criminals, organizations can better prepare themselves to detect, prevent, and respond to cyber threats. Utilizing threat intelligence, proactive monitoring, and collaboration among stakeholders will enhance the ability to anticipate and mitigate risks in an increasingly complex digital landscape. As cybercriminals continue to evolve their tactics, staying informed about these patterns is critical for maintaining robust cybersecurity defenses.

7.2 Techniques for Tracking Online Threat Actors: Following breadcrumbs from phishing, fraud, and other attacks.

In the landscape of cybercrime, understanding the techniques used to track online threat actors is essential for cybersecurity professionals, law enforcement, and researchers. These individuals often leave behind digital breadcrumbs that can be followed to uncover their identities, motivations, and future actions. This section explores effective techniques for tracking online threat actors, focusing on phishing, fraud, and other cybercrimes.

1. Understanding Online Threat Actors

Online threat actors encompass a wide range of individuals or groups engaged in malicious activities, including cybercriminals, hacktivists, state-sponsored actors, and opportunistic fraudsters. Each of these entities operates with varying motivations, methodologies, and levels of sophistication, making tracking their activities a multifaceted challenge.

1.1 Types of Threat Actors

- **Cybercriminals**: Often motivated by financial gain, these actors engage in activities such as phishing, ransomware attacks, and identity theft.
- **Hacktivists**: Individuals or groups that hack for political or social causes, often targeting organizations they perceive as unethical.
- **State-Sponsored Actors**: Operate on behalf of a government and may engage in espionage, sabotage, or information warfare.

2. Following Breadcrumbs: Key Techniques

To effectively track online threat actors, investigators can employ various techniques to analyze the digital traces left behind during cyberattacks.

2.1 Analyzing Phishing Attacks

Phishing attacks are a common method employed by cybercriminals to harvest sensitive information. Analyzing these attacks can yield valuable information about threat actors.

Email Header Analysis: The email header contains metadata about the sender and the path the email took. By examining the "Received" fields, investigators can trace the email back to its origin and potentially identify the sender's IP address.

- Steps for Email Header Analysis:
- Obtain the email header from the email client.
- Identify the originating IP address from the header.

Use IP lookup tools (like IPinfo or Whois) to gather additional information about the sender.

URL and Link Inspection: Phishing emails often contain malicious links that redirect users to fake websites. Inspecting these URLs can reveal the underlying domain and hosting information.

Use of URL Unshortening Tools: Services like Unshorten.me can help reveal the true destination of shortened links, providing insights into the sites being used in the attack.

Malware Domain Analysis: Tools such as VirusTotal can be used to check the reputation of the domains linked in phishing emails.

2.2 Tracking Fraudulent Activities

Fraud can take many forms, from credit card fraud to online scams. Tracking these activities requires a multifaceted approach.

Identifying Common Patterns: Analyzing the methods used in fraud schemes can help identify potential threats. For instance, fraudsters may target specific demographics or use similar communication styles.

Analysis of Reported Incidents: Reviewing reports from victims can help establish patterns in fraud attempts, such as common email addresses, phone numbers, or tactics used.

Social Media and Online Marketplace Monitoring: Many fraudsters operate on platforms like eBay, Craigslist, or social media. Monitoring these platforms can help identify fraudulent listings and users.

Using Keyword Alerts: Setting up alerts for specific keywords or phrases associated with fraud can help catch potential scams early.

Community Reporting: Engaging with community forums or platforms (like Reddit or Scamwatch) allows victims to report fraud attempts and share information.

2.3 Leveraging OSINT Tools

Open Source Intelligence (OSINT) tools play a critical role in tracking online threat actors. By utilizing these tools, investigators can aggregate and analyze data from various sources.

Maltego: A powerful OSINT tool that helps visualize relationships between different entities. It can analyze data from social media, websites, and other sources to uncover connections between threat actors.

Utilizing Entity Recognition: Maltego can automatically identify and map entities such as domains, email addresses, and social media profiles, making it easier to see potential links between them.

Shodan: A search engine for internet-connected devices that can reveal vulnerabilities. Investigators can use Shodan to locate compromised devices that may be associated with threat actors.

Search for Specific Vulnerabilities: Querying Shodan with keywords related to known vulnerabilities can help locate potentially compromised systems used by threat actors.

Censys: Similar to Shodan, Censys provides a comprehensive view of internet-connected devices and services. It can help trace the infrastructure used by cybercriminals.

3. Analyzing Online Behavior

Tracking online threat actors also involves understanding their behavior patterns and online interactions.

3.1 Digital Footprints

Threat actors often leave digital footprints that can be analyzed to gather intelligence.

Social Media Analysis: Many cybercriminals engage in discussions on forums or social media platforms. By monitoring these discussions, investigators can uncover intentions and tactics.

Identifying Unique Usernames: Threat actors may use consistent usernames across platforms, making it easier to track their activities.

Forum Monitoring: Cybercriminal forums often serve as a marketplace for illegal services. Monitoring these forums can provide insights into emerging threats and tactics.

Using Web Scraping Tools: Tools like Beautiful Soup or Scrapy can help automate the extraction of information from forums and websites where cybercriminals congregate.

3.2 Behavioral Analysis

Analyzing the behavior of threat actors can provide insights into their methods and motivations.

Identifying Tactics, Techniques, and Procedures (TTPs): By analyzing past incidents, investigators can identify common TTPs used by threat actors, allowing for better predictions of future attacks.

Building Threat Models: Creating threat models based on observed behaviors can help organizations prepare defenses against similar attacks.

4. Collaboration and Information Sharing

Effective tracking of online threat actors often requires collaboration among various stakeholders.

4.1 Information Sharing Platforms

Engaging in information-sharing platforms can enhance collective knowledge about threats and tactics:

Participating in Cybersecurity Alliances: Organizations like Information Sharing and Analysis Centers (ISACs) facilitate the sharing of threat intelligence among industries.

Utilizing Threat Intelligence Feeds: Subscribing to threat intelligence feeds can keep organizations informed about emerging threats and tactics used by cybercriminals.

4.2 Law Enforcement Collaboration

Collaboration with law enforcement agencies can be essential for tracking and apprehending online threat actors.

Reporting Incidents: Victims of cybercrime should report incidents to local law enforcement, which can facilitate investigations and share information with national and international agencies.

Engaging with Cybercrime Units: Many countries have specialized cybercrime units that can provide expertise and resources for tracking online threat actors.

Tracking online threat actors requires a comprehensive approach that combines technical analysis, behavioral insights, and collaborative efforts. By following the digital breadcrumbs left behind in phishing, fraud, and other attacks, investigators can piece together valuable intelligence that informs cybersecurity strategies and helps apprehend cybercriminals. The ongoing evolution of cyber threats necessitates a proactive stance, leveraging tools, methodologies, and partnerships to stay one step ahead of those who exploit the digital landscape for malicious purposes. As cybercriminals continue to adapt their tactics, the ability to track and understand their behavior becomes increasingly vital for ensuring cybersecurity and protecting individuals and organizations from harm.

7.3 Case Studies in Cybercrime Detection: Real-world examples of OSINT used to prevent or investigate cybercrimes.

Open Source Intelligence (OSINT) has become an indispensable tool in the fight against cybercrime. By leveraging publicly available information, cybersecurity professionals, law enforcement agencies, and researchers can uncover patterns, detect threats, and ultimately prevent or investigate cybercrimes. This section presents several compelling case studies that highlight the effectiveness of OSINT in real-world scenarios.

1. Case Study 1: The Capture of the Dark Web Drug Trafficker

Overview: In 2017, the U.S. Drug Enforcement Administration (DEA) used OSINT techniques to track down a prominent dark web drug dealer known as "Dread Pirate Roberts" who was operating on Silk Road 2.0. The suspect was implicated in selling various illegal substances, including opioids.

OSINT Techniques Employed:

Username Analysis: Investigators began by examining the online persona of the suspect, focusing on his usernames, which were consistently used across multiple forums and marketplaces.

Digital Footprint Mapping: They analyzed the suspect's digital footprint, including forum posts, transaction histories, and associated email addresses. They discovered connections between the suspect's usernames and his real-world identity through cross-referencing data on social media platforms.

Social Media Monitoring: Investigators monitored the suspect's social media activities for clues. Posts related to his lifestyle, interests, and interactions provided valuable insights into his whereabouts and associates.

Outcome: The combined OSINT efforts led to the identification of the suspect's physical location. The DEA successfully arrested him, ultimately dismantling a significant drug trafficking operation. This case demonstrated the power of OSINT in tracing online identities to real-world locations.

2. Case Study 2: The Discovery of a Phishing Operation

Overview: In 2018, a collaborative effort between the Cybersecurity and Infrastructure Security Agency (CISA) and cybersecurity firms revealed a large-scale phishing operation targeting multiple organizations across the United States.

OSINT Techniques Employed:

Email Header Analysis: Investigators analyzed thousands of phishing emails to trace their origins. By examining email headers, they identified several IP addresses that were repeatedly used in the phishing campaigns.

Domain Analysis: The team performed WHOIS lookups on the domains used in the phishing emails, revealing common registration details that linked multiple phishing domains to a single registrar.

Pattern Recognition: By examining the content and structure of the phishing emails, investigators identified recurring phrases and techniques, helping to categorize them as part of a coordinated campaign.

Outcome: The investigation resulted in the shutdown of numerous phishing domains and the identification of several individuals involved in the operation. This case highlighted the importance of email analysis and domain tracking as effective OSINT techniques for combating phishing.

3. Case Study 3: Uncovering a Ransomware Attack

Overview: In 2020, a major ransomware attack targeted a healthcare provider, compromising sensitive patient data and disrupting operations. The incident prompted an extensive investigation using OSINT to trace the origins of the attack.

OSINT Techniques Employed:

Analyzing Ransom Note: The ransomware operators left a ransom note with specific instructions. Investigators used the language, formatting, and payment demands to trace the group's previous activities and tactics.

Dark Web Monitoring: Researchers monitored dark web forums and marketplaces for discussions about the attack. They identified postings by individuals claiming responsibility, discussing the tactics used, and even auctioning off stolen data.

Geolocation Techniques: By analyzing metadata from the ransomware and related communications, investigators were able to trace some of the operational infrastructure back to specific geographic locations known for hosting cybercriminal activities.

Outcome: This OSINT-driven investigation led to the identification of the ransomware group and the recovery of some of the stolen data. It also provided insights into the group's methodologies, allowing cybersecurity teams to better defend against similar attacks in the future.

4. Case Study 4: Preventing Financial Fraud

Overview: In 2021, a financial institution faced a series of fraudulent activities involving stolen credit cards. The bank collaborated with law enforcement to investigate the fraudulent transactions using OSINT techniques.

OSINT Techniques Employed:

Transaction Analysis: Investigators analyzed patterns in the fraudulent transactions to identify commonalities in the locations, IP addresses, and timestamps of the fraud attempts.

Social Media Scrutiny: By monitoring social media, investigators discovered several posts by individuals boasting about their fraudulent activities, which included selling stolen credit card information.

Reverse IP Lookup: The use of reverse IP lookup tools helped trace the IP addresses back to hosting services known for being used by cybercriminals, providing leads on potential suspects.

Outcome: The investigation led to the identification and apprehension of several individuals involved in the fraudulent scheme. The case underscored the importance of transaction analysis and social media monitoring in preventing financial fraud.

5. Case Study 5: Tracking a Cyber Espionage Group

Overview: In 2019, a prominent cybersecurity firm investigated a series of cyberattacks attributed to a suspected state-sponsored group known for espionage activities. The firm employed OSINT to gather evidence and track the group's operations.

OSINT Techniques Employed:

Infrastructure Mapping: Investigators analyzed the digital infrastructure used in the attacks, including the IP addresses and domains involved, to map out the group's operational network.

Behavioral Analysis: By studying previous attacks linked to the group, researchers identified specific tactics, techniques, and procedures (TTPs) that helped in predicting their next move.

Media Monitoring: The team monitored international news sources and cyber threat intelligence reports to gather insights into the group's motivations and affiliations.

Outcome: The investigation provided critical insights into the group's methods and potential targets, allowing organizations to strengthen their defenses. This case illustrated how OSINT can be vital in tracking state-sponsored cyber espionage.

These case studies highlight the diverse applications of OSINT in detecting, preventing, and investigating cybercrimes. By utilizing various techniques—from analyzing digital footprints to monitoring dark web activities—cybersecurity professionals can effectively track threat actors and mitigate the impact of cybercrime. As cyber threats continue to evolve, the importance of OSINT as a powerful tool in the cybersecurity arsenal will only grow. Through collaboration, technology, and innovative analysis, organizations can stay ahead of cybercriminals and protect their digital assets more effectively.

Chapter 8: Data Collection from the Deep and Dark Web

Chapter 8, Data Collection from the Deep and Dark Web, uncovers the unique challenges and opportunities presented by these hidden corners of the internet. This chapter explains the distinctions between the surface web, deep web, and dark web, and guides readers on safely navigating these areas using specialized tools and techniques. Readers will learn about the types of data and information that can be found on the deep and dark web, such as illicit marketplaces, forums, and unindexed databases. The chapter emphasizes the importance of anonymity and security precautions when accessing these sites, covering best practices for maintaining privacy. Additionally, it discusses the ethical and legal considerations involved in collecting data from these sources. By the end of this chapter, readers will be equipped with the knowledge to conduct effective and responsible research in the deep and dark web, expanding their OSINT toolkit significantly.

8.1 Understanding the Deep and Dark Web: What differentiates the surface, deep, and dark web and how to access them.

The internet is often viewed as a single entity, but it is actually comprised of multiple layers, each serving distinct purposes and offering varying degrees of accessibility. This layered architecture can be broadly categorized into three segments: the surface web, the deep web, and the dark web. Understanding the differences between these layers is crucial for anyone interested in Open Source Intelligence (OSINT), cybersecurity, or digital privacy. This section delves into these layers, their characteristics, and how to access the deep and dark web safely and effectively.

1. The Surface Web

Definition: The surface web is the portion of the internet that is indexed by standard search engines like Google, Bing, and Yahoo. It consists of publicly accessible websites that can be easily found and accessed without any special tools or permissions.

Characteristics:

- **Accessibility**: The surface web is readily available to anyone with an internet connection and a web browser.
- **Content**: It includes websites, blogs, news articles, social media platforms, and other resources that are openly accessible.
- **Size**: While the surface web is substantial, it is only a small fraction of the entire internet, estimated to constitute about 4% to 10% of all online content.

Examples:

- Social media sites (Facebook, Twitter)
- News websites (CNN, BBC)
- E-commerce platforms (Amazon, eBay)

2. The Deep Web

Definition: The deep web encompasses all parts of the internet that are not indexed by traditional search engines. This includes content that is behind paywalls, password-protected sites, private databases, and any other information that requires specific access credentials to view.

Characteristics:

- **Accessibility**: Accessing deep web content typically requires a username and password or specific permissions. Standard search engines cannot index this content.
- **Content**: It includes databases, academic journals, corporate intranets, government resources, and any private information not meant for public consumption.
- **Size**: The deep web is estimated to be hundreds of times larger than the surface web, with estimates suggesting it could contain 90% or more of all online content.

Examples:

- Online banking sites
- Medical databases (e.g., PubMed)
- Academic resources (e.g., JSTOR)

3. The Dark Web

Definition: The dark web is a small segment of the deep web that has been intentionally hidden and is inaccessible through standard web browsers. It requires specific software, configurations, or authorization to access.

Characteristics:

- **Anonymity**: The dark web is designed to provide anonymity to both users and website operators. This is achieved through various technologies, with Tor being the most popular.
- **Content**: It contains a mix of legal and illegal activities, including forums for whistleblowers, illegal drug sales, counterfeit currency, hacking services, and other illicit content.
- **Access**: Accessing the dark web typically involves using specific software, such as Tor or I2P, which routes traffic through multiple servers to mask user identity and location.

Examples:

- Dark web marketplaces (e.g., Silk Road, AlphaBay)
- Whistleblower platforms (e.g., SecureDrop)
- Anonymity-focused forums (e.g., The Hub)

4. Accessing the Deep and Dark Web

Understanding how to safely navigate the deep and dark web is critical, especially for OSINT practitioners, researchers, and individuals concerned about privacy.

4.1 Accessing the Deep Web

Accessing the deep web is often straightforward, as it generally involves logging into platforms or databases that require specific credentials. Here are some general guidelines:

- **Use Secure Passwords**: Always employ strong, unique passwords for accounts that access deep web resources.
- **VPN Services**: Utilize Virtual Private Networks (VPNs) to add an extra layer of security and privacy while accessing sensitive information.
- **Trusted Sources**: Ensure that the websites or databases accessed are reputable to avoid scams or data breaches.

4.2 Accessing the Dark Web

Accessing the dark web requires specific software and precautions to ensure user safety and anonymity. Here's a step-by-step guide:

Download Tor Browser: The most common method to access the dark web is through the Tor browser. Tor allows users to access .onion sites that are not available on the surface web. Download Tor from the official website to avoid malicious versions.

Use a VPN: Before opening Tor, consider using a VPN for additional privacy. This helps mask your IP address from both your Internet Service Provider (ISP) and any potential surveillance.

Stay Anonymous: When using the dark web, avoid revealing personal information. Use pseudonyms and never disclose identifying details.

Be Cautious of Links: Dark web links often have a .onion suffix and can be easily shared in forums. Exercise caution when clicking links, as many can lead to malicious sites.

Avoid Illegal Activities: While the dark web can provide access to valuable resources, it is also home to many illegal activities. Engaging in these can lead to severe legal consequences.

Security Tools: Consider using additional security tools such as malware scanners and encrypted communication platforms to protect your data and interactions.

Understanding the differences between the surface web, deep web, and dark web is crucial for effectively navigating the internet, especially for those involved in OSINT and cybersecurity. While the surface web is easily accessible and familiar, the deep and dark web offer valuable resources and information that can be essential for research and investigation. However, accessing these layers requires caution, awareness of legal implications, and an understanding of the technologies involved. By following best practices and remaining vigilant, individuals can effectively leverage the deep and dark web for their objectives while minimizing risks.

8.2 Safely Navigating Dark Web Sources: Tools and precautions for accessing dark web marketplaces and forums.

Navigating the dark web can be a daunting task, primarily due to its association with illegal activities, anonymity, and the potential for encountering malicious content. However, for researchers, cybersecurity professionals, and those interested in Open Source Intelligence (OSINT), the dark web also offers valuable insights, information, and data that may not be available elsewhere. This section provides guidance on the tools and precautions necessary for safely accessing dark web marketplaces and forums.

1. Understanding the Risks

Before diving into the tools and precautions, it is essential to recognize the inherent risks of navigating the dark web:

- **Legal Consequences**: Engaging in illegal activities, such as purchasing illicit goods or services, can lead to severe legal repercussions.
- **Malware and Scams**: Many dark web sites are designed to exploit users, whether through malware distribution, phishing attempts, or scams.
- **Anonymity Breaches**: Even though the dark web provides a degree of anonymity, it is still possible for skilled adversaries or law enforcement to trace users back to their real identities if proper precautions are not taken.

2. Essential Tools for Dark Web Navigation

2.1 Tor Browser

The Tor browser is the primary tool for accessing the dark web. It allows users to navigate .onion sites, which are specific to the dark web and not indexed by traditional search engines.

- **Installation**: Download the Tor browser from the official Tor Project website to avoid malicious versions. Ensure that your antivirus is updated and running before installation.
- **Configuration**: Follow the setup prompts and choose the option to connect to the Tor network. The browser is pre-configured to maintain user anonymity.

2.2 VPN (Virtual Private Network)

Using a VPN in conjunction with Tor adds an extra layer of privacy by masking your IP address from your ISP and potential adversaries.

- **Choosing a VPN**: Select a reputable VPN provider that does not log user activity. Some recommended VPNs for dark web use include ExpressVPN, NordVPN, and ProtonVPN.
- **Connecting**: Connect to the VPN before launching the Tor browser to ensure that all traffic is encrypted and your real IP address is hidden.

2.3 Secure Operating Systems

Using a secure operating system can enhance security when accessing the dark web. Consider utilizing:

- **Tails OS**: Tails is a live operating system that runs from a USB stick, designed for anonymity and privacy. It routes all internet connections through the Tor network and leaves no trace on the host computer.
- **Whonix**: Whonix is a privacy-focused operating system that uses Tor and is built to protect against IP leaks and other threats.

2.4 Secure Communication Tools

For communicating on dark web forums or marketplaces, consider using encrypted messaging applications like:

- **Signal**: An encrypted messaging app that provides end-to-end encryption for messages and calls.
- **PGP (Pretty Good Privacy):** A data encryption standard used to secure emails and messages. It's useful for maintaining confidentiality when communicating sensitive information.

3. Precautions for Safe Navigation

Navigating the dark web requires careful consideration and a proactive approach to security. Here are several precautions to take:

3.1 Maintain Anonymity

- **Avoid Personal Information**: Do not disclose any personal information that could be used to identify you, such as your name, address, or phone number.
- **Use Pseudonyms**: When engaging in forums or marketplaces, use pseudonyms or aliases instead of your real identity.

3.2 Assessing Websites

- **Verify Links**: Be cautious with links and URLs. Use forums like the "Hidden Wiki" to find reliable links to dark web sites, as they often curate safer links.
- **Check for HTTPS**: Always look for HTTPS in the URL. While not foolproof, it can indicate that the site takes security seriously.

3.3 Use Malware Protection

- **Install Antivirus Software**: Ensure that you have updated antivirus software running on your device to help detect and block malicious activity.
- **Regular Scans**: Conduct regular scans of your system for malware, especially after visiting dark web sites.

3.4 Limit Your Exposure

- **Use a Dedicated Device**: Consider using a separate computer or device exclusively for accessing the dark web. This can help isolate any potential threats from your primary device.
- **Avoid Downloads**: Refrain from downloading files from dark web sites, as they may contain malware or other harmful content.

3.5 Be Aware of Scams

- **Recognize Common Scams**: Be aware of common dark web scams, such as fake marketplaces or sellers who take payment but fail to deliver goods.
- **Research Sellers and Services**: Before engaging in any transactions, research sellers and services on forums to see if they have positive reviews or a history of successful trades.

The dark web offers valuable resources for those willing to navigate its complexities, but it also poses significant risks. By employing the right tools and adhering to precautions, users can safely access dark web marketplaces and forums for research, OSINT, or cybersecurity purposes. Always prioritize your safety and privacy, maintain anonymity, and be vigilant against potential threats. By understanding the dark web and using it responsibly, individuals can uncover hidden information while minimizing risks and legal consequences.

8.3 Ethical and Legal Challenges: Balancing information gathering with the risks and laws associated with dark web use.

The dark web is a complex and multifaceted environment that presents unique opportunities for information gathering, particularly in fields such as cybersecurity, law enforcement, and intelligence. However, the ethical and legal challenges associated with accessing and using dark web resources are significant. Navigating this space requires a careful balance between the benefits of information gathering and the potential legal repercussions and ethical dilemmas that can arise. This section explores the ethical and legal considerations inherent in dark web use and offers guidance for responsible navigation.

1. Understanding the Dark Web's Dual Nature

The dark web serves as both a platform for illicit activities and a space for legitimate purposes, such as:

Illicit Activities: The dark web is notorious for facilitating illegal transactions, including the sale of drugs, weapons, stolen data, and hacking services. It also hosts forums for cybercriminals and other individuals engaged in unlawful behavior.

Legitimate Uses: Conversely, the dark web can also serve as a haven for whistleblowers, activists, and journalists seeking to communicate securely and anonymously. It provides a platform for free speech in oppressive regimes, where individuals face censorship or persecution.

Understanding this dual nature is crucial for individuals and organizations seeking to navigate the dark web responsibly.

2. Legal Challenges

2.1 Jurisdictional Issues

One of the primary legal challenges associated with dark web use is the issue of jurisdiction. The global nature of the internet means that actions taken in one country may have legal implications in another. This can create confusion about which laws apply:

Varying Laws: Different countries have different laws governing privacy, data protection, and cybercrime. What may be legal in one jurisdiction could be illegal in another, leading to potential legal ramifications for users.

Enforcement Difficulties: Law enforcement agencies may face challenges in pursuing investigations across borders due to varying legal standards and cooperative agreements between nations.

2.2 Criminal Liability

Engaging in illegal activities on the dark web can expose individuals to significant legal risks. Common concerns include:

Purchasing Illegal Goods: Buying illegal items, such as drugs or weapons, can result in criminal charges. Even if the transaction is unsuccessful, attempting to purchase illegal goods may lead to prosecution.

Accessing Stolen Data: Downloading or accessing stolen data, such as credit card information or personal identification, can constitute a crime, exposing users to civil liability or criminal charges.

Participating in Forums: Engaging in discussions or activities that promote illegal behavior can also lead to legal consequences, as law enforcement agencies monitor dark web forums for illicit activities.

3. Ethical Challenges

3.1 Informed Consent

Gathering information from the dark web raises ethical questions surrounding informed consent, particularly when it comes to user privacy:

Anonymous Users: Many individuals who post on dark web forums or sell goods do so under the assumption of anonymity. Collecting and using their information without consent can violate ethical principles and privacy rights.

Exploitation of Vulnerable Populations: The dark web often contains content that exploits vulnerable individuals, such as victims of human trafficking or those involved in illegal activities out of desperation. Researchers must consider the ethical implications of using such information.

3.2 Harmful Activities

Navigating the dark web can inadvertently contribute to harmful activities, whether through negligence or intentional actions:

Facilitating Crime: Sharing or utilizing information from dark web sources may inadvertently aid in criminal activities, such as cybercrime or trafficking, leading to ethical concerns about complicity.

Promoting Illegal Behavior: Engaging with dark web communities that promote illegal behavior can normalize harmful activities and undermine the legal and ethical standards society upholds.

3.3 The Responsibility of Researchers

For those conducting research or gathering intelligence from the dark web, ethical considerations extend to the responsibility of the researcher:

Transparency: Researchers must be transparent about their intentions and methodologies when collecting data from the dark web, ensuring that their actions are ethical and justified.

Public Good: The motivation behind gathering information should prioritize the public good and contribute to a greater understanding of the challenges posed by dark web activities, rather than personal gain or sensationalism.

4. Best Practices for Ethical and Legal Navigation

To balance information gathering with the ethical and legal challenges of dark web use, individuals and organizations can follow these best practices:

4.1 Conduct Thorough Research

Before accessing dark web sources, conduct thorough research on the legal implications and ethical considerations involved. Understanding the specific laws in your jurisdiction can help mitigate legal risks.

4.2 Seek Legal Counsel

For organizations or individuals engaged in extensive research or intelligence-gathering activities, seeking legal counsel can provide clarity on the legal landscape and ensure compliance with applicable laws.

4.3 Develop Ethical Guidelines

Establishing clear ethical guidelines for engaging with dark web content can help navigate the complex moral landscape. These guidelines should address issues of informed consent, the treatment of vulnerable populations, and the responsibility of researchers.

4.4 Maintain Anonymity and Security

When navigating the dark web, prioritize anonymity and security to minimize the risks of legal repercussions and potential harm. Use secure tools and practices to protect your identity and data.

4.5 Focus on Constructive Use

Aim to use information gathered from the dark web for constructive purposes, such as enhancing cybersecurity measures, supporting law enforcement, or contributing to academic research that promotes understanding of the challenges associated with dark web activities.

Navigating the dark web presents significant ethical and legal challenges that require careful consideration and responsible practices. By understanding the complexities of the dark web's dual nature and prioritizing ethical standards, individuals and organizations can effectively balance information gathering with the risks and laws associated with dark web use. Through informed decision-making, transparency, and a commitment to the public good, it is possible to responsibly engage with this hidden segment of the internet while minimizing potential legal repercussions and ethical dilemmas.

Chapter 9: Automated Data Mining and Scripting for OSINT

Chapter 9, Automated Data Mining and Scripting for OSINT, focuses on the use of automation and scripting to enhance the efficiency and effectiveness of open-source intelligence gathering. This chapter introduces readers to programming basics, particularly in Python, and highlights its application in automating repetitive OSINT tasks such as data collection, analysis, and reporting. Readers will explore various data mining techniques, including web scraping, which allows them to extract information from websites quickly and systematically. The chapter also discusses the importance of APIs and how to leverage them to gather real-time data from various online platforms, such as social media and news outlets. By the end of this chapter, readers will have the skills to create simple scripts and automated workflows that significantly streamline their OSINT efforts, enabling them to focus on higher-level analysis and interpretation of the gathered data.

9.1 Introduction to Python for OSINT: Basics of Python scripting to automate data collection.

In the world of Open Source Intelligence (OSINT), the ability to efficiently collect, analyze, and visualize data is crucial for success. One of the most effective ways to enhance your OSINT capabilities is through automation, and Python has emerged as a powerful tool for this purpose. This section introduces the basics of Python scripting for OSINT, focusing on how Python can be leveraged to automate data collection and streamline your investigative workflows.

1. Why Python for OSINT?

Python has become a go-to programming language for many OSINT professionals due to its versatility, ease of use, and extensive libraries. Here are some key reasons why Python is ideal for OSINT tasks:

Simplicity and Readability: Python's syntax is straightforward and easy to understand, making it accessible for both beginners and experienced programmers. This simplicity allows OSINT practitioners to focus more on solving problems rather than struggling with complex code.

Rich Ecosystem of Libraries: Python boasts a wealth of libraries and frameworks specifically designed for data collection, analysis, and visualization. Popular libraries include requests for making HTTP requests, Beautiful Soup for web scraping, and Pandas for data manipulation.

Community Support: The Python community is vast and active, providing a wealth of resources, tutorials, and forums where users can seek help and share knowledge. This collaborative environment fosters learning and innovation.

2. Setting Up Your Python Environment

Before diving into Python scripting for OSINT, you'll need to set up your development environment. Follow these steps to get started:

2.1 Install Python

- **Download Python**: Visit the official Python website (python.org) and download the latest version of Python suitable for your operating system (Windows, macOS, or Linux).
- **Install Python**: Follow the installation instructions. During installation, make sure to check the option to add Python to your system PATH.

2.2 Set Up a Code Editor

Choose a code editor or Integrated Development Environment (IDE) for writing your Python scripts. Some popular options include:

- **Visual Studio Code**: A lightweight and powerful editor with a rich set of extensions.
- **PyCharm**: A robust IDE specifically designed for Python development, offering advanced features like code completion and debugging.
- **Jupyter Notebook**: An interactive environment that allows you to create and share documents containing live code, equations, visualizations, and narrative text.

2.3 Install Necessary Libraries

You can install Python libraries using pip, the Python package installer. Open your command prompt or terminal and run the following commands to install essential libraries for OSINT:

```
pip install requests
pip install beautifulsoup4
pip install pandas
pip install matplotlib
```

- **requests**: A library for making HTTP requests to access web resources.
- **Beautiful Soup**: A library for parsing HTML and XML documents, making it easy to scrape data from web pages.
- **Pandas**: A powerful data manipulation and analysis library, useful for handling structured data.
- **Matplotlib**: A plotting library that allows you to create static, interactive, and animated visualizations in Python.

3. Basic Python Scripting Concepts

Before automating OSINT tasks, it's essential to understand some fundamental Python concepts:

3.1 Variables and Data Types

In Python, you can store data in variables, which can hold different data types, including:

- **Strings**: Text data enclosed in quotes (e.g., "Hello, World!").
- **Integers**: Whole numbers (e.g., 42).
- **Floats**: Decimal numbers (e.g., 3.14).
- **Lists**: Ordered collections of items (e.g., [1, 2, 3, 4]).
- **Dictionaries**: Key-value pairs for storing data (e.g., {"name": "John", "age": 30}).

3.2 Control Structures

Control structures allow you to control the flow of your program. Key structures include:

Conditionals: Using if, elif, and else statements to execute code based on certain conditions.

```
if age >= 18:
    print("Adult")
else:
    print("Minor")
```

Loops: Using for and while loops to repeat actions.

```
for i in range(5):
    print(i)
```

3.3 Functions

Functions are reusable blocks of code that perform a specific task. You can define a function using the def keyword:

```
def greet(name):
    return f"Hello, {name}!"

print(greet("Alice"))
```

4. Example: Automating Data Collection with Python

Now that you have a basic understanding of Python, let's look at a simple example of how to use Python for data collection in an OSINT context. This example demonstrates how to scrape data from a website using requests and Beautiful Soup.

4.1 Web Scraping Example

In this example, we'll scrape the titles of articles from a sample news website.

```
import requests
from bs4 import BeautifulSoup

# Step 1: Send an HTTP request to the website
url = "https://example-news-website.com"
response = requests.get(url)

# Step 2: Parse the HTML content
soup = BeautifulSoup(response.content, 'html.parser')

# Step 3: Extract article titles
titles = soup.find_all('h2', class_='article-title')

# Step 4: Print the titles
for title in titles:
```

print(title.text)

4.2 Explanation of the Code

- **Import Libraries**: Import the requests and Beautiful Soup libraries to handle HTTP requests and HTML parsing.
- **Send Request**: Use requests.get(url) to send an HTTP GET request to the specified URL.
- **Parse HTML**: Create a BeautifulSoup object to parse the HTML content of the response.
- **Extract Data**: Use soup.find_all() to find all <h2> elements with the class article-title, which contains the article titles.
- **Print Results**: Loop through the extracted titles and print them.

Python scripting offers OSINT practitioners a powerful way to automate data collection and analysis. By leveraging libraries like requests and Beautiful Soup, users can efficiently gather and process information from various online sources, enhancing their investigative capabilities. As you continue to explore Python for OSINT, consider delving into more advanced topics, such as data visualization, machine learning, and API integrations, to further enhance your skills and effectiveness in this dynamic field. With Python in your toolkit, you'll be well-equipped to tackle the challenges of modern OSINT investigations.

9.2 Data Scraping Techniques: Using web scraping to gather data efficiently from open sources.

In the realm of Open Source Intelligence (OSINT), data scraping is a crucial technique that allows practitioners to extract information from websites and online platforms. This process enables the efficient collection of valuable data from a variety of sources, such as social media, news sites, forums, and public databases. In this section, we will explore the fundamentals of web scraping, including techniques, best practices, and ethical considerations to ensure effective and responsible data gathering.

1. What is Web Scraping?

Web scraping is the automated process of extracting information from web pages. By utilizing programming tools and libraries, users can collect structured data from HTML content, which can then be analyzed for various purposes, including research, monitoring, and investigation.

Key Characteristics of Web Scraping:

- **Automation**: Web scraping allows for the automated extraction of data, reducing the time and effort required for manual collection.
- **Structured Data**: The goal is to convert unstructured data (such as text or images on a web page) into structured formats (like CSV or JSON) that can be easily analyzed and processed.
- **Scalability**: Web scraping can be performed on a large scale, enabling the collection of data from multiple sources simultaneously.

2. Common Web Scraping Techniques

To effectively gather data from open sources, it's important to understand various web scraping techniques. Below are some of the most commonly used methods:

2.1 Basic HTML Parsing

The simplest form of web scraping involves downloading the HTML content of a webpage and parsing it to extract relevant information.

Tools: Libraries like Beautiful Soup (Python) and Cheerio (JavaScript) are commonly used for parsing HTML content.

Process:

- Send an HTTP request to the target URL.
- Retrieve the HTML response.
- Use parsing libraries to navigate the HTML structure and locate specific elements.

Example:

```
import requests
from bs4 import BeautifulSoup

url = "https://example.com"
response = requests.get(url)
soup = BeautifulSoup(response.text, 'html.parser')
```

```
data = soup.find_all('div', class_='data-class')

for item in data:
    print(item.text)
```

2.2 Using APIs

Many websites offer Application Programming Interfaces (APIs) that provide structured data in a more accessible format, often in JSON or XML. Utilizing APIs is generally more efficient and less error-prone than web scraping.

Advantages:

- APIs usually provide structured and up-to-date data.
- They reduce the risk of being blocked or facing legal issues associated with scraping.

Example: To access Twitter data, you can use the Twitter API to gather tweets, user profiles, and other relevant information.

2.3 Browser Automation

For dynamic websites that rely on JavaScript to load content, traditional scraping techniques may not suffice. Browser automation tools can simulate human interaction with a webpage to extract data.

Tools: Selenium, Puppeteer, and Playwright are popular libraries for browser automation.

Process:

- Launch a web browser through the automation tool.
- Navigate to the desired webpage.

Interact with elements (like clicking buttons or filling out forms) to load the necessary data.

Example:

```
from selenium import webdriver

driver = webdriver.Chrome()
```

```
driver.get("https://example.com")
data = driver.find_element_by_class_name('data-class').text
print(data)
driver.quit()
```

2.4 Scraping from Multiple Pages

To collect data from websites that paginate their content, you can automate the navigation through multiple pages to gather comprehensive datasets.

Process:

- Identify the pattern in the URL for pagination (e.g., ?page=2).
- Loop through the pages, sending requests and extracting data from each one.

Example:

```
for page in range(1, 6):  # Scraping the first 5 pages
    url = f"https://example.com/articles?page={page}"
    response = requests.get(url)
    soup = BeautifulSoup(response.text, 'html.parser')
    articles = soup.find_all('h2', class_='article-title')
    for article in articles:
        print(article.text)
```

3. Best Practices for Web Scraping

To ensure efficient and responsible web scraping, it's essential to adhere to best practices:

3.1 Respect Robots.txt

Most websites provide a robots.txt file that specifies which parts of the site can be crawled by automated agents. Always check this file to respect the website's scraping policies.

Example: You can view the robots.txt file by appending /robots.txt to the website's URL (e.g., https://example.com/robots.txt).

3.2 Rate Limiting

To avoid overwhelming a server and getting blocked, implement rate limiting by introducing delays between requests. This mimics human browsing behavior and reduces the risk of detection.

Example:

```
import time

for url in urls:
    response = requests.get(url)
    # Process the response
    time.sleep(1)  # Wait for 1 second before the next request
```

3.3 Error Handling

Incorporate error handling mechanisms to gracefully handle unexpected issues, such as network errors, HTTP errors, or changes in website structure.

Example:

```
try:
    response = requests.get(url)
    response.raise_for_status()  # Raise an error for bad responses
except requests.exceptions.RequestException as e:
    print(f"Error occurred: {e}")
```

3.4 Storing Data

Decide how to store the extracted data. Common formats include CSV, JSON, or databases like SQLite. Ensure your storage solution is efficient and easy to access for further analysis.

Example: Storing scraped data in a CSV file:

```
import pandas as pd

data = {'Title': titles, 'Link': links}
df = pd.DataFrame(data)
df.to_csv('scraped_data.csv', index=False)
```

4. Ethical Considerations

While web scraping is a powerful tool, it's essential to navigate the ethical landscape responsibly:

- **Consent**: Always consider whether you have the right to scrape the data. Even if it is publicly accessible, users may expect their data to be private.
- **Impact**: Consider the potential impact of your scraping activities on the target website. Excessive scraping can lead to degraded service for regular users.
- **Transparency**: Be transparent about your data collection practices, especially if the data will be used for research, reporting, or analysis.

Web scraping is a vital technique in OSINT that enables the efficient collection of data from open sources. By utilizing various scraping techniques, adhering to best practices, and considering ethical implications, practitioners can leverage web scraping to gather valuable insights for their investigations. As you delve deeper into web scraping, continuous learning and adaptation will be key to effectively navigating the dynamic landscape of online information. By mastering these techniques, you will enhance your OSINT capabilities and become a more effective cyber sleuth.

9.3 API Integrations for OSINT: Leveraging APIs from services like Twitter, Google Maps, and others to collect intelligence.

In the rapidly evolving field of Open Source Intelligence (OSINT), the integration of Application Programming Interfaces (APIs) is transforming the way data is collected and analyzed. APIs allow OSINT practitioners to access structured and often real-time data from various online platforms and services. This section explores the importance of APIs in OSINT, how to leverage them effectively, and examples of popular APIs used for intelligence gathering.

1. Understanding APIs in OSINT

An API is a set of rules and protocols that allows different software applications to communicate with each other. APIs provide a standardized way to access data and services from external platforms, enabling users to integrate and utilize this data within their applications.

Benefits of Using APIs in OSINT:

- **Structured Data**: APIs often return data in structured formats like JSON or XML, making it easier to parse and analyze.
- **Real-Time Access**: APIs can provide real-time data updates, essential for monitoring and timely intelligence gathering.
- **Reduced Complexity**: By using APIs, practitioners can bypass the complexities of web scraping, such as handling HTML parsing and dealing with website changes.
- **Enhanced Reliability**: APIs are typically more reliable than scraping methods, which may fail if the website's structure changes or if the site implements anti-scraping measures.

2. Key APIs for OSINT

Several APIs offer valuable data that can be harnessed for OSINT purposes. Here are some notable examples:

2.1 Twitter API

The Twitter API allows users to access Twitter data, including tweets, user profiles, hashtags, and trends. This is particularly useful for gathering sentiment analysis, tracking conversations, and monitoring public opinion on various topics.

Common Use Cases:

- Tracking specific hashtags or keywords to gauge public sentiment.
- Collecting tweets related to specific events or topics for analysis.
- Monitoring user interactions to identify influencers or networks.

Example:

```
import tweepy

# Authenticate to Twitter
auth = tweepy.OAuthHandler('API_KEY', 'API_SECRET')
auth.set_access_token('ACCESS_TOKEN', 'ACCESS_TOKEN_SECRET')
api = tweepy.API(auth)

# Collect tweets containing a specific hashtag
```

```
tweets = api.search(q="#OpenSourceIntelligence", count=100)

for tweet in tweets:
    print(f"{tweet.user.name}: {tweet.text}")
```

2.2 Google Maps API

The Google Maps API provides geolocation and mapping services that can be invaluable for OSINT investigations. It allows users to access geographic data, visualize locations, and even perform geocoding (converting addresses into geographic coordinates).

Common Use Cases:

- Mapping the locations of specific events or incidents.
- Analyzing geographic trends related to a particular subject.
- Visualizing routes and distances between locations for planning investigations.

Example:

```
import googlemaps

# Authenticate to Google Maps
gmaps = googlemaps.Client(key='YOUR_API_KEY')

# Geocode an address
geocode_result = gmaps.geocode("1600 Amphitheatre Parkway, Mountain View, CA")

for result in geocode_result:
    print(result['formatted_address'])
```

2.3 OpenWeatherMap API

The OpenWeatherMap API provides access to weather data, which can be useful for contextualizing events and understanding environmental factors that may influence investigations.

Common Use Cases:

- Monitoring weather conditions during significant events (e.g., protests, disasters).

- Analyzing weather patterns that could impact logistics for operations or investigations.

Example:

```
import requests

# Fetch weather data for a specific city
response =
requests.get('http://api.openweathermap.org/data/2.5/weather?q=London&appid=YOUR
_API_KEY')
weather_data = response.json()

print(f"Current temperature in London: {weather_data['main']['temp']}K")
```

2.4 YouTube Data API

The YouTube Data API allows users to access video content, comments, and user information on the platform. This can be useful for analyzing trends in video content, understanding public opinion, and monitoring events.

Common Use Cases:

- Tracking video uploads related to specific topics or incidents.
- Analyzing comments for sentiment or public reaction to content.

Example:

```
from googleapiclient.discovery import build

# Authenticate to YouTube API
youtube = build('youtube', 'v3', developerKey='YOUR_API_KEY')

# Search for videos by keyword
request = youtube.search().list(q='Open Source Intelligence', part='snippet',
type='video', maxResults=5)
response = request.execute()

for item in response['items']:
    print(f"Title: {item['snippet']['title']}, Channel: {item['snippet']['channelTitle']}")
```

3. Best Practices for Using APIs in OSINT

To maximize the effectiveness of API integrations in your OSINT efforts, consider the following best practices:

3.1 Authentication and Access

Most APIs require authentication to access their data. Familiarize yourself with the authentication methods used by the API (e.g., API keys, OAuth) and ensure that you follow the necessary procedures to obtain access.

3.2 Rate Limiting

APIs often impose rate limits on the number of requests you can make within a specific timeframe. Monitor your usage to avoid exceeding these limits, which could lead to temporary bans or throttled access.

3.3 Data Handling and Storage

Develop a strategy for storing and managing the data collected from APIs. This may involve saving data in databases, spreadsheets, or other formats, depending on your analysis needs.

3.4 Compliance with Terms of Service

Always review the terms of service for any API you use. Ensure that your data collection methods comply with their guidelines to avoid potential legal issues.

4. Ethical Considerations

When leveraging APIs for OSINT, it's crucial to navigate ethical considerations responsibly:

- **User Privacy**: Respect the privacy of individuals whose data you are accessing. Be aware of the implications of collecting and using personal data.
- **Transparency**: If your work involves public reporting or dissemination of collected data, maintain transparency about your data sources and methods.
- **Purpose Limitation**: Use the data collected from APIs only for legitimate purposes that align with ethical guidelines and legal standards.

API integrations are a powerful asset in the OSINT toolkit, allowing practitioners to access structured, real-time data from various online platforms. By leveraging APIs like Twitter, Google Maps, OpenWeatherMap, and YouTube, you can enhance your intelligence-gathering capabilities and gain deeper insights into events and trends. As you explore API usage for OSINT, keep in mind the importance of ethical considerations and best practices to ensure responsible data collection and analysis. With the right approach, API integrations can significantly improve your efficiency and effectiveness as a cyber sleuth in the ever-evolving landscape of open source intelligence.

Chapter 10: Analyzing and Visualizing OSINT Data

Chapter 10, Analyzing and Visualizing OSINT Data, delves into the crucial processes of interpreting and presenting the information collected through open-source intelligence. This chapter begins by outlining key data analysis techniques that help transform raw data into meaningful insights, emphasizing the importance of data cleaning and organization. Readers will learn how to use various analytical tools and software to identify patterns, trends, and anomalies within their data sets. The chapter also highlights the significance of data visualization, showcasing tools like Gephi, Tableau, and Maltego to create compelling visual representations of complex information. By illustrating connections, relationships, and geographic distributions, these visualizations enhance understanding and communication of findings to stakeholders. By the end of this chapter, readers will be equipped with both analytical and visualization skills, enabling them to produce clear, actionable intelligence reports that effectively convey their OSINT discoveries.

10.1 Introduction to Data Analysis for OSINT: How to prepare and clean data for analysis.

Data analysis is a critical component of Open Source Intelligence (OSINT) as it transforms raw data into actionable insights. However, before any meaningful analysis can take place, data must be prepared and cleaned to ensure accuracy, relevance, and usability. This section introduces the essential steps involved in preparing and cleaning data specifically for OSINT purposes, highlighting techniques and best practices that practitioners can apply to enhance their analytical processes.

1. Understanding the Importance of Data Preparation and Cleaning

Data preparation and cleaning are foundational steps in the data analysis workflow. In OSINT, the data collected from various sources can be messy, inconsistent, and incomplete. Proper preparation ensures that the analysis is based on high-quality data, which leads to more reliable conclusions and insights.

Key Benefits of Data Preparation and Cleaning:

- **Improved Accuracy**: Cleaning data helps eliminate errors and inconsistencies, leading to more accurate results.
- **Enhanced Efficiency**: Well-prepared data can significantly reduce the time spent on analysis, allowing for quicker decision-making.
- **Increased Relevance**: By filtering out irrelevant information, analysts can focus on data that directly contributes to their objectives.

2. Steps in Data Preparation and Cleaning

Data preparation and cleaning for OSINT typically involve several key steps:

2.1 Data Collection

The first step involves gathering data from various open sources. This could include social media platforms, websites, databases, and other online repositories. It's essential to document the sources of data for transparency and future reference.

Techniques: Data can be collected through web scraping, API integrations, or manual downloads, depending on the nature of the source.

2.2 Data Assessment

Once data is collected, the next step is to assess its quality. This involves examining the data for completeness, accuracy, and consistency. Analysts should ask themselves:

- Are there missing values in the dataset?
- Are there duplicates or redundant entries?
- Is the data consistent in terms of format and representation?

Example: When collecting data from social media, check if all tweets are in the same language and if timestamps are standardized.

2.3 Data Cleaning

Data cleaning involves several tasks aimed at rectifying issues identified during the assessment phase. Common cleaning techniques include:

Handling Missing Values: Decide how to deal with missing data points. Options include removing records with missing values, imputing values based on statistical methods, or flagging them for further investigation.

Example: If a user profile lacks location data, you could impute it with the average location of similar users or leave it as is with a flag indicating missing data.

Removing Duplicates: Identify and remove duplicate entries to ensure that each data point is unique.

Example:

import pandas as pd

 # Load the dataset
data = pd.read_csv('osint_data.csv')

 # Remove duplicate rows
data_cleaned = data.drop_duplicates()

Standardizing Formats: Ensure consistency in data formats, such as date formats (e.g., converting all dates to ISO 8601 format) and text casing (e.g., converting all strings to lowercase).

Example:

 # Standardize date format
data_cleaned['date'] = pd.to_datetime(data_cleaned['date']).dt.strftime('%Y-%m-%d')

Correcting Errors: Identify and correct errors in the data, such as typos, incorrect values, or misclassified information.

Example: If a dataset includes a column for country names, you may find variations like "USA" and "United States." Consolidating these into a single representation improves data integrity.

Filtering Irrelevant Data: Remove data points that do not contribute to the analysis or that fall outside the desired parameters.

Example: If you're analyzing tweets related to a specific event, you may want to exclude tweets that contain unrelated hashtags or keywords.

2.4 Data Transformation

After cleaning, the next step is to transform the data into a suitable format for analysis. This may involve:

Creating New Variables: Generate new variables that could provide additional insights. For example, deriving sentiment scores from text data using natural language processing (NLP) techniques.

Example:

```
from textblob import TextBlob

# Calculate sentiment score
data_cleaned['sentiment'] = data_cleaned['text'].apply(lambda x:
TextBlob(x).sentiment.polarity)
```

Normalizing Data: Adjusting data to a common scale, particularly when dealing with numerical data from different sources. Normalization helps in making comparisons easier and more meaningful.

Aggregating Data: Combining multiple records into summary statistics (e.g., averaging, counting) to facilitate analysis.

2.5 Data Storage

Once the data is cleaned and transformed, it should be stored in a suitable format for analysis. Common storage solutions include:

Databases: SQL or NoSQL databases can efficiently store large datasets and facilitate complex queries.

Data Files: CSV, Excel, or JSON files may be appropriate for smaller datasets or when sharing data with others.

Example:

```
# Save cleaned data to a new CSV file
data_cleaned.to_csv('cleaned_osint_data.csv', index=False)
```

3. Tools for Data Preparation and Cleaning

Several tools and libraries can assist in data preparation and cleaning tasks:

Pandas: A powerful Python library for data manipulation and analysis, particularly useful for handling tabular data.

OpenRefine: A web-based tool for working with messy data, allowing users to explore, clean, and transform datasets.

Excel: A widely used spreadsheet tool that provides various functions for data cleaning and analysis.

4. Challenges in Data Preparation and Cleaning

Despite its importance, data preparation and cleaning can be challenging due to:

Data Volume: Large datasets may require significant processing time and resources.

Data Diversity: Data collected from different sources may have varying formats and structures, complicating the cleaning process.

Dynamic Data: For real-time OSINT applications, data may change frequently, necessitating ongoing cleaning and preparation.

Preparing and cleaning data for OSINT analysis is a vital process that significantly impacts the quality of insights derived from data. By following systematic steps—ranging from data collection and assessment to cleaning and transformation—OSINT practitioners can ensure they are working with high-quality data. This foundation not only enhances the efficiency of analysis but also leads to more accurate and relevant intelligence outcomes. In an age where data is abundant, mastering these techniques is essential for effective and responsible OSINT practices.

10.2 Visualizing Connections and Patterns: Using tools like Maltego and Gephi to visualize relationships and trends.

In the realm of Open Source Intelligence (OSINT), data visualization plays a crucial role in interpreting complex datasets and revealing relationships and patterns that may not be immediately apparent. Effective visualization can help analysts communicate their findings clearly and support decision-making processes. This section explores two powerful tools—Maltego and Gephi—used for visualizing connections and patterns within OSINT data, along with best practices for utilizing them effectively.

1. The Importance of Data Visualization in OSINT

Data visualization allows analysts to transform raw data into graphical representations, making it easier to identify trends, patterns, and outliers. This is particularly valuable in OSINT, where large volumes of diverse data must be interpreted to draw meaningful conclusions.

Key Benefits of Data Visualization:

- **Enhanced Understanding**: Visuals simplify complex data, making it more accessible and easier to comprehend for both analysts and stakeholders.
- **Pattern Recognition**: Graphical representations help highlight relationships and patterns that might go unnoticed in textual data, enabling more informed analysis.
- **Storytelling**: Visualizations can tell a story, guiding viewers through data narratives that illustrate the significance of the findings.
- **Informed Decision-Making**: Well-designed visualizations support strategic decisions by presenting clear, actionable insights based on the data.

2. Using Maltego for Visualization

Maltego is a powerful OSINT tool designed for link analysis and data mining. It allows users to visualize relationships between various data points, such as people, organizations, domains, and more. Maltego's unique graph-based approach makes it an invaluable resource for investigators and analysts.

Key Features of Maltego:

- **Entity Types**: Maltego supports various entity types, including persons, emails, phone numbers, domains, and social media accounts, allowing users to create comprehensive visualizations.
- **Transforms**: Maltego utilizes "transforms" to pull data from multiple sources and create connections between entities automatically. Users can visualize how different entities relate to one another in real time.
- **Graph Visualization**: The tool provides a visual interface that displays connections between entities, making it easy to identify patterns and relationships.

How to Use Maltego for Visualization:

Data Input: Begin by adding entities relevant to your investigation (e.g., a domain name, a person's name, or an email address) to a new graph in Maltego.

Applying Transforms: Utilize Maltego's transforms to gather data about the entities and create connections. For instance, applying a transform on an email address can reveal associated social media accounts or domains.

Visual Analysis: As connections are created, analyze the graph to identify clusters, outliers, and significant relationships. Maltego allows for dynamic interaction with the graph, enabling users to explore relationships further.

Exporting Visualizations: Once analysis is complete, export the visualization as an image or PDF for reporting purposes or presentations.

Example Use Case: A cybersecurity analyst might use Maltego to investigate a phishing attack. By inputting the email address used in the phishing attempt, the analyst can visualize connections to other email addresses, domains, and social media accounts, revealing a broader network of potential malicious activity.

3. Using Gephi for Network Visualization

Gephi is an open-source network visualization and analysis tool designed for exploring and visualizing complex networks. It is especially powerful for visualizing large datasets and understanding the structure and dynamics of networks.

Key Features of Gephi:

- **Graph Layout Algorithms**: Gephi offers various layout algorithms to arrange nodes in a way that highlights the underlying structure of the network (e.g., ForceAtlas2, Fruchterman-Reingold).
- **Data Exploration**: Users can interactively explore the network, zooming in and out, filtering nodes and edges based on specific criteria, and manipulating the layout to emphasize particular patterns.
- **Statistical Analysis**: Gephi includes tools for calculating network statistics, such as centrality measures, clustering coefficients, and community detection, helping analysts uncover insights from the data.

How to Use Gephi for Visualization:

Data Import: Import your dataset into Gephi. The data should be formatted in a way that defines nodes (e.g., individuals, organizations) and edges (relationships between nodes).

Graph Creation: Once the data is imported, Gephi will create a visual representation of the network. Nodes will represent entities, while edges will indicate relationships.

Applying Layouts: Use the various layout algorithms to arrange the network visually. This can help identify clusters or communities within the data.

Filtering and Exploration: Filter nodes and edges based on specific attributes (e.g., degree of connection, type of relationship) to focus on relevant parts of the network.

Exporting Visualizations: After analysis, export the network visualization for reports or presentations in various formats (PNG, PDF, etc.).

Example Use Case: A journalist investigating human trafficking networks could use Gephi to visualize connections between known traffickers, victims, and their locations. By analyzing the network structure, they can identify key players and patterns, informing their investigative approach.

4. Best Practices for Visualization in OSINT

To maximize the effectiveness of data visualization in OSINT, consider the following best practices:

- **Define Clear Objectives**: Before visualizing data, determine what you aim to convey. A clear objective helps focus your analysis and design choices.
- **Choose the Right Tool**: Select a visualization tool that best fits your needs. Maltego is ideal for relationship mapping, while Gephi excels at large network analysis.
- **Simplify Visuals**: Avoid cluttered visuals. Use colors, shapes, and sizes to emphasize important information while maintaining clarity.
- **Interactive Elements**: Where possible, incorporate interactive elements that allow users to explore the data further, enhancing engagement and understanding.
- **Documentation**: Document your visualization process, including the sources of data and the methods used. This transparency enhances the credibility of your analysis.

Visualizing connections and patterns is a fundamental aspect of data analysis in OSINT. Tools like Maltego and Gephi empower analysts to uncover relationships and trends hidden within complex datasets. By leveraging these tools effectively, OSINT practitioners can enhance their investigative capabilities, ultimately leading to more informed decisions and strategic actions. As data continues to grow in complexity and volume, mastering visualization techniques will be essential for effective OSINT practices in today's digital landscape.

10.3 Creating Intelligence Reports: Best practices for creating clear, actionable OSINT reports.

In the field of Open Source Intelligence (OSINT), producing clear and actionable intelligence reports is crucial for conveying findings to stakeholders and decision-makers. A well-structured report not only summarizes the data and insights gathered but also provides context, recommendations, and implications for action. This section outlines best practices for creating effective OSINT reports that enhance communication and facilitate informed decision-making.

1. The Importance of Intelligence Reports

Intelligence reports serve as the primary medium for sharing insights derived from OSINT analysis. These reports transform complex data into digestible information, allowing stakeholders to understand the implications of findings and make informed decisions based on them. Effective reporting can also help prioritize actions and allocate resources more efficiently.

Key Benefits of Intelligence Reports:

- **Enhanced Communication**: Clear reports improve communication between analysts and stakeholders, ensuring everyone is aligned on findings and recommendations.
- **Actionable Insights**: Well-crafted reports provide specific, actionable recommendations that guide decision-making processes.
- **Documentation**: Reports serve as a documented history of investigations, providing a reference for future analyses and decisions.

2. Structuring an OSINT Intelligence Report

A well-structured intelligence report typically includes several key components. Each section should serve a specific purpose and contribute to the overall clarity and effectiveness of the report.

2.1 Executive Summary

The executive summary provides a high-level overview of the report's key findings and recommendations. It should be concise, typically one page or less, and highlight the most critical insights.

- **Purpose**: To give readers a quick understanding of the report without delving into details.
- **Content**: Summarize the main findings, implications, and recommended actions.

2.2 Introduction

The introduction sets the stage for the report, providing context for the analysis and outlining the objectives of the investigation.

- **Purpose**: To explain the background of the investigation and its significance.
- **Content**: Include details about the focus of the OSINT inquiry, the sources of data used, and the key questions the report seeks to answer.

2.3 Methodology

The methodology section describes the approach taken to gather and analyze data. This transparency helps establish credibility and allows readers to understand how conclusions were drawn.

- **Purpose**: To provide insight into the analytical process and the reliability of findings.
- **Content**: Detail the tools and techniques used for data collection and analysis, any limitations encountered, and how data was verified.

2.4 Findings

The findings section presents the core insights derived from the OSINT analysis. This part of the report should be organized logically, using headings and subheadings to guide the reader.

- **Purpose**: To convey the results of the analysis clearly and effectively.
- **Content**: Use bullet points, tables, or charts to present data visually where appropriate, and include qualitative insights alongside quantitative data.

Example:

- **Finding 1**: Identification of key individuals involved in a cyber incident, along with their social media profiles and connections.
- **Finding 2**: Detection of common patterns in phishing attacks related to the investigated domain.

2.5 Analysis and Interpretation

In this section, provide an analysis of the findings, interpreting the data in the context of the original objectives. This is where analysts can discuss implications, trends, and potential consequences of the findings.

- **Purpose**: To contextualize the findings and provide insights into their significance.
- **Content**: Discuss how the findings relate to the broader landscape, highlight any risks or opportunities, and provide a deeper understanding of the implications.

2.6 Recommendations

The recommendations section outlines specific actions stakeholders should consider based on the findings. This part should be clear, actionable, and prioritized where possible.

- **Purpose**: To guide stakeholders on potential next steps based on the intelligence provided.
- **Content**: Use bullet points or numbered lists for clarity, and ensure each recommendation is directly tied to findings from the analysis.

The conclusion summarizes the key points made throughout the report and reinforces the importance of the findings and recommendations.

- **Purpose**: To wrap up the report and reinforce the main takeaways.
- **Content**: Briefly restate the significance of the analysis and the urgency of the recommendations, if applicable.

2.8 Appendices

If applicable, include appendices for supplementary materials, such as raw data, detailed methodologies, or additional resources.

- **Purpose**: To provide additional context or information without cluttering the main report.
- **Content**: Include any detailed data, charts, or references that support the findings and analysis.

3. Best Practices for Creating OSINT Intelligence Reports

To ensure the effectiveness of OSINT intelligence reports, consider the following best practices:

3.1 Use Clear and Concise Language

Avoid jargon and overly technical language that may confuse readers. Use clear, straightforward language to ensure that the report is accessible to all stakeholders.

3.2 Tailor the Report to Your Audience

Consider the knowledge level and interests of the report's audience. Customize the content and level of detail based on whether the report is intended for technical experts, executives, or general stakeholders.

3.3 Utilize Visuals Effectively

Incorporate charts, graphs, and tables to present data visually. Visuals can enhance understanding and retention, making it easier for readers to grasp complex information quickly.

3.4 Ensure Accurate Citations and References

Clearly cite sources of information and data throughout the report. Proper citations enhance credibility and allow readers to verify information.

3.5 Review and Edit Thoroughly

Before finalizing the report, conduct a thorough review for clarity, accuracy, and completeness. Consider having a peer review the report to provide feedback and identify any areas for improvement.

3.6 Use a Consistent Format

Maintain a consistent format throughout the report, including fonts, headings, and spacing. A professional appearance enhances readability and credibility.

Creating clear, actionable OSINT intelligence reports is vital for effective communication and informed decision-making. By structuring reports thoughtfully and adhering to best practices, analysts can ensure that their findings are presented in a manner that resonates with stakeholders and drives meaningful actions. In an age where information is abundant, the ability to distill complex data into clear, actionable insights will set effective OSINT practitioners apart, ultimately contributing to more robust security and strategic initiatives.

Chapter 11: Case Studies and Real-World OSINT Applications

Chapter 11, Case Studies and Real-World OSINT Applications, presents a collection of compelling examples that demonstrate how open-source intelligence has been effectively utilized across various fields. This chapter features detailed case studies from law enforcement, corporate security, and investigative journalism, showcasing the diverse applications of OSINT in real-world scenarios. Readers will learn about high-profile investigations where OSINT played a pivotal role in solving crimes, mitigating security threats, and verifying information in the media. Each case study highlights specific techniques and tools used, providing practical insights into the OSINT process in action. By examining these real-life examples, readers will gain a deeper understanding of the potential impact of OSINT, as well as best practices and lessons learned that they can apply in their own investigative efforts. This chapter ultimately reinforces the value of OSINT as a vital resource for professionals seeking to navigate today's complex digital landscape effectively.

11.1 OSINT in Law Enforcement and Security: Examples of OSINT used in criminal investigations.

Open Source Intelligence (OSINT) has become an invaluable asset for law enforcement and security agencies worldwide. By leveraging publicly available information, these organizations can enhance their investigative capabilities, solve crimes more effectively, and prevent potential threats. This section explores how OSINT is utilized in various criminal investigations, highlighting real-world examples and illustrating its significance in modern law enforcement.

1. The Role of OSINT in Law Enforcement

OSINT encompasses the collection and analysis of information obtained from publicly available sources, including social media, news articles, public records, forums, and more. In law enforcement, OSINT serves several critical functions:

- **Crime Prevention**: By monitoring online activities and trends, law enforcement agencies can identify potential criminal behavior before it escalates.

- **Investigative Support**: OSINT can provide leads and background information during investigations, helping officers build profiles and understand the context of criminal activities.
- **Situational Awareness**: OSINT enhances situational awareness by providing real-time information about ongoing incidents, public sentiment, and emerging threats.
- **Collaboration**: OSINT can facilitate collaboration between agencies and organizations, enabling the sharing of information and insights across jurisdictions.

2. Real-World Examples of OSINT in Criminal Investigations

2.1 Missing Persons Cases

One of the most notable applications of OSINT in law enforcement is in missing persons investigations. For instance, in 2019, authorities in California utilized OSINT techniques to locate a missing girl. Investigators monitored social media platforms and public forums where users were discussing the case. They identified crucial leads and potential sightings reported by community members. Through targeted outreach and the analysis of user-generated content, law enforcement was able to generate credible leads that ultimately led to the girl's safe recovery.

2.2 Human Trafficking

OSINT plays a pivotal role in combating human trafficking. Law enforcement agencies leverage various online resources to identify and track trafficking networks. In one case, investigators in Texas used OSINT tools to analyze advertisements on classified sites known for facilitating sex trafficking. By tracking IP addresses and cross-referencing ads with known traffickers, they could identify patterns and connections among individuals involved in the trafficking operation. This intelligence led to multiple arrests and the rescue of victims.

2.3 Cybercrime Investigations

OSINT is also instrumental in investigating cybercrime. For example, in a case involving a phishing scheme targeting thousands of individuals, law enforcement agencies employed OSINT tools to analyze phishing emails and websites. By examining domain registration information, social media accounts, and forum discussions, investigators were able to identify the perpetrators behind the scheme. The use of OSINT not only aided in the arrest of the criminals but also helped recover stolen funds and prevent further attacks.

2.4 Terrorism Prevention

Preventing terrorist activities is another area where OSINT proves invaluable. Law enforcement agencies monitor social media platforms and online forums to detect early signs of radicalization and extremist behavior. In 2020, during the COVID-19 pandemic, authorities noted an increase in online extremist activity as groups sought to exploit public fears and unrest. By analyzing social media posts and discussions, law enforcement could identify potential threats and intervene before any acts of violence occurred.

One notable example occurred in the United Kingdom, where the UK's Counter Terrorism Policing (CTP) unit employed OSINT to monitor extremist chatter online. Through diligent analysis of posts on social media, they identified individuals expressing intent to engage in violent acts. This intelligence led to preemptive actions that disrupted planned attacks and prevented potential casualties.

2.5 Fraud Investigations

OSINT is a critical tool in investigating various types of fraud, including identity theft and financial scams. For example, in a case involving fraudulent loan applications, investigators utilized OSINT techniques to trace the digital footprints of the suspects. They analyzed publicly available records, social media profiles, and online reviews to piece together the suspects' activities and connections.

By cross-referencing data from multiple sources, investigators uncovered a network of individuals collaborating in the scheme. This led to coordinated arrests and a broader investigation that revealed a much larger fraudulent operation.

3. Tools and Techniques Used in OSINT Investigations

Law enforcement agencies employ a range of tools and techniques to collect and analyze OSINT effectively. Some popular tools include:

- **Social Media Monitoring Tools**: Tools like Hootsuite, Meltwater, and Mention allow agencies to track conversations, keywords, and trends across social media platforms.
- **Geolocation Tools**: Services such as Google Earth and ArcGIS enable investigators to analyze location-based data, helping them track suspects and map out crime scenes.

- **Data Aggregation Tools**: Platforms like Maltego and Palantir can consolidate information from various public sources, creating comprehensive profiles of individuals and networks.

By utilizing these tools, law enforcement agencies can enhance their investigative efforts, making informed decisions based on actionable intelligence.

4. Challenges and Considerations

While OSINT offers numerous advantages for law enforcement, there are also challenges and ethical considerations that must be addressed:

- **Data Overload**: The vast amount of information available online can lead to data overload. Analysts must be skilled at filtering and prioritizing data to extract meaningful insights.
- **Privacy Concerns**: Investigators must navigate legal and ethical boundaries when collecting OSINT. Respecting individual privacy rights while gathering information is essential to maintain public trust.
- **Information Validity**: Not all information obtained through OSINT is reliable. Analysts must critically assess sources and verify data to avoid drawing erroneous conclusions.

OSINT has transformed the landscape of law enforcement and security, providing agencies with powerful tools to enhance their investigative capabilities. By utilizing publicly available information, law enforcement can solve crimes more efficiently, prevent potential threats, and improve community safety. As technology and online platforms continue to evolve, the importance of OSINT in criminal investigations will only grow, necessitating ongoing training, adaptation, and ethical considerations in its application.

11.2 OSINT for Corporate Security and Reputation Management: Case studies on corporate applications of OSINT.

Open Source Intelligence (OSINT) has increasingly become a vital component of corporate security and reputation management strategies. Companies utilize publicly available information to identify potential threats, monitor brand reputation, and mitigate risks associated with their operations. This section explores the application of OSINT in the corporate sector through notable case studies, demonstrating how organizations effectively leverage this intelligence to safeguard their interests.

1. The Role of OSINT in Corporate Security

In the corporate world, OSINT plays several crucial roles, including:

- **Threat Identification**: Detecting potential security threats, such as data breaches or insider threats, before they escalate.
- **Risk Assessment**: Evaluating external risks that could impact business operations, including geopolitical events, regulatory changes, or competitive actions.
- **Reputation Management**: Monitoring online sentiment related to the brand, products, and services to maintain a positive corporate image.
- **Competitive Intelligence**: Gathering insights on competitors' activities, market trends, and consumer behavior to inform strategic decisions.

2. Case Studies of OSINT in Corporate Security

2.1 Target's Data Breach Investigation

In 2013, Target Corporation suffered a massive data breach that exposed the personal information of approximately 40 million customers. Following the incident, the company employed OSINT strategies to understand the breach's scope and assess its potential impact on brand reputation.

- **OSINT Application**: Target's security team monitored online forums and social media platforms for discussions related to the breach. By analyzing public sentiment and customer feedback, they identified key concerns and misinformation circulating online.
- **Outcome**: The insights gained through OSINT allowed Target to address customer concerns promptly and transparently, improving its crisis communication strategy. They implemented a robust public relations campaign to reassure customers, which helped restore trust in the brand over time.

2.2 McDonald's Monitoring Negative Sentiment

In 2017, McDonald's faced a public relations crisis when a social media campaign, #McDStories, went awry, leading to a flood of negative tweets about the company's food quality and customer service. The fast-food giant quickly turned to OSINT to manage the situation.

- **OSINT Application**: McDonald's utilized social media monitoring tools to track mentions of the hashtag and analyze public sentiment in real-time. They assessed which topics were driving negative sentiment and which customer complaints were most frequent.
- **Outcome**: With insights from OSINT, McDonald's launched a proactive response campaign, addressing customer complaints and showcasing improvements in food quality. This swift action helped to mitigate the damage to the brand's reputation and restored positive engagement on social media.

2.3 Sony Pictures Entertainment Cyberattack

In 2014, Sony Pictures Entertainment fell victim to a devastating cyberattack that resulted in the leak of sensitive information, including unreleased films and private employee data. Following the attack, the company turned to OSINT to enhance its corporate security posture.

- **OSINT Application**: Sony Pictures' security team utilized OSINT tools to monitor online forums and dark web marketplaces for discussions about the leaked data and any potential threats related to ongoing projects. They also analyzed media reports to gauge public reaction and the effectiveness of their damage control efforts.
- **Outcome**: Through OSINT, Sony Pictures identified potential insider threats and reassessed their cybersecurity protocols. They implemented a more robust incident response strategy and enhanced employee training on cybersecurity awareness, which significantly improved their resilience against future attacks.

3. Case Studies of OSINT in Reputation Management

3.1 Nestlé's Corporate Social Responsibility (CSR) Monitoring

Nestlé, a multinational food and beverage company, has faced criticism over its sourcing practices and environmental impact. To manage its reputation, the company actively monitors public sentiment related to its CSR initiatives.

- **OSINT Application**: Nestlé employed OSINT tools to track conversations about its sustainability efforts across social media platforms, blogs, and news outlets. By identifying key influencers and sentiment trends, the company could engage with critics and respond to misinformation effectively.

- **Outcome**: This proactive approach allowed Nestlé to adjust its CSR messaging and communication strategies, resulting in improved public perception and a stronger brand reputation.

3.2 Airbnb's Response to Regulatory Challenges

Airbnb has faced significant scrutiny from local governments and communities over its impact on housing markets and urban neighborhoods. To navigate these challenges, the company employs OSINT to monitor public sentiment and regulatory developments.

- **OSINT Application**: Airbnb uses OSINT tools to track discussions on social media, forums, and news articles related to short-term rentals. This monitoring helps the company identify regulatory trends and community concerns in real-time.
- **Outcome**: By leveraging OSINT insights, Airbnb can proactively engage with stakeholders, address concerns, and advocate for favorable regulations. This approach has enabled the company to build stronger relationships with local communities and improve its reputation as a responsible business.

4. Tools and Techniques Used in Corporate OSINT

Companies utilize a variety of tools and techniques to collect and analyze OSINT effectively, including:

- **Social Media Monitoring Platforms**: Tools like Brandwatch, Hootsuite, and Sprout Social enable organizations to track brand mentions, sentiment, and emerging trends across social media platforms.
- **News Aggregators**: Services such as Google Alerts and Feedly allow companies to monitor news coverage and industry developments in real-time.
- **Data Analytics Tools**: Tools like Tableau and Power BI help businesses visualize and analyze OSINT data, uncovering trends and insights that inform strategic decisions.

5. Challenges and Considerations

While OSINT provides significant benefits to corporate security and reputation management, challenges exist:

- **Data Quality and Reliability**: The vast amount of information available can include misinformation or unreliable sources. Companies must establish methods for verifying data credibility.
- **Privacy Concerns**: Organizations must navigate legal and ethical considerations when collecting and analyzing public data, ensuring compliance with privacy regulations.
- **Information Overload**: The sheer volume of data can lead to analysis paralysis. Companies need effective filtering and prioritization techniques to extract actionable insights.

OSINT has become a critical component of corporate security and reputation management, enabling organizations to monitor threats, manage crises, and enhance stakeholder engagement. Through the examination of case studies, it is evident that proactive OSINT strategies can significantly influence a company's ability to respond to challenges and safeguard its reputation. As technology evolves and the information landscape expands, businesses that effectively leverage OSINT will be better positioned to navigate risks and maintain a competitive edge in their respective industries.

11.3 OSINT in Journalism and Media: How journalists use OSINT to verify sources and uncover stories.

Open Source Intelligence (OSINT) has transformed the landscape of journalism and media, providing reporters with powerful tools to verify sources, uncover hidden stories, and hold the powerful accountable. As traditional journalism grapples with misinformation and the rapid spread of news, OSINT serves as a crucial ally in ensuring accuracy and integrity. This section explores the applications of OSINT in journalism through various case studies, illustrating how reporters leverage publicly available information to enhance their investigative efforts.

1. The Role of OSINT in Journalism

OSINT encompasses the collection and analysis of publicly available data, which journalists use for various purposes:

- **Source Verification**: Ensuring the credibility of sources and information before publishing stories.
- **Fact-Checking**: Cross-referencing claims made by individuals or organizations against verified data to ensure accuracy.

- **Investigative Research**: Digging deeper into stories by gathering information from social media, public records, and other open sources.
- **Contextual Understanding**: Providing background information and context to help audiences better understand complex issues.

2. Case Studies of OSINT in Journalism

2.1 The Syrian Civil War Reporting

During the Syrian Civil War, journalists faced significant challenges in verifying information and ensuring the accuracy of their reports amid a chaotic and rapidly evolving situation. OSINT played a crucial role in their efforts.

- **OSINT Application**: Journalists utilized satellite imagery and social media platforms to corroborate claims made by both the government and opposition groups. By analyzing images from platforms like Twitter and Instagram, they could verify the locations and events described in reports. Additionally, they employed geolocation techniques to pinpoint the time and place of videos and images shared online.
- **Outcome**: This approach enabled journalists to provide a more accurate account of events, dispelling misinformation and offering critical insights into the humanitarian crisis. By validating claims through OSINT, they enhanced their credibility and built trust with their audience.

2.2 Investigating the 2016 U.S. Presidential Election

The 2016 U.S. Presidential Election was marked by rampant misinformation and foreign interference. Journalists relied heavily on OSINT to investigate claims of fake news and the origins of disinformation campaigns.

- **OSINT Application**: Reporters used OSINT techniques to analyze the social media activity of political campaigns, identifying patterns of misinformation and tracking the sources of fake news stories. By tracing the origins of posts and analyzing engagement metrics, journalists could uncover coordinated disinformation efforts from foreign entities and domestic sources.
- **Outcome**: The findings from these investigations led to important revelations about the role of social media in the election, informing the public and prompting discussions about media literacy and the need for greater accountability in the digital age.

2.3 Uncovering Corruption with Data Journalism

Data journalism has emerged as a powerful tool for investigative reporters, and OSINT plays a pivotal role in this field. A notable example is the work of the International Consortium of Investigative Journalists (ICIJ) in the Panama Papers investigation.

- **OSINT Application**: The ICIJ utilized OSINT techniques to analyze a massive leak of documents detailing offshore financial activities. Journalists combined data from public records, corporate registries, and social media profiles to track connections between prominent figures and their offshore accounts. They cross-referenced data with existing databases to identify potential corruption and illicit activities.
- **Outcome**: The Panama Papers investigation led to significant global revelations about tax evasion and corruption, prompting resignations, policy changes, and calls for greater transparency in financial systems. The effective use of OSINT was instrumental in bringing these issues to light.

2.4 Investigating Human Rights Abuses

Journalists reporting on human rights abuses often face challenges in verifying claims made by victims and organizations. OSINT can help provide critical context and corroborate testimonies.

- **OSINT Application**: In investigating allegations of human rights abuses in Myanmar, journalists employed OSINT techniques to analyze satellite imagery and social media posts from affected areas. They used geolocation tools to verify the timing and authenticity of videos depicting violence against civilians, ensuring that their reports were based on factual evidence.
- **Outcome**: The insights gained through OSINT allowed journalists to produce comprehensive reports that shed light on the situation in Myanmar, contributing to international awareness and advocacy for human rights protections.

3. Tools and Techniques Used in Journalistic OSINT

Journalists employ a variety of OSINT tools and techniques to enhance their reporting efforts, including:

- **Social Media Analysis Tools**: Platforms like TweetDeck, Crowdtangle, and Brandwatch help journalists track trends and monitor public sentiment related to ongoing stories.

- **Geolocation Tools**: Services such as Google Earth, ArcGIS, and various satellite imagery platforms allow journalists to analyze locations and events in real-time.
- **Fact-Checking Websites**: Tools like Snopes, FactCheck.org, and PolitiFact provide resources for verifying claims made by public figures and organizations.
- **Public Records Databases**: Journalists utilize databases such as PACER (Public Access to Court Electronic Records) and OpenSecrets.org to access court filings and campaign finance data.

4. Challenges and Considerations

While OSINT offers significant advantages for journalists, challenges exist:

- **Information Overload**: The abundance of available information can make it difficult for journalists to sift through and identify relevant data. Establishing effective filtering techniques is crucial.
- **Verification Difficulties**: With the rise of deepfakes and manipulated media, verifying the authenticity of visual content has become increasingly complex.
- **Legal and Ethical Boundaries**: Journalists must navigate legal and ethical considerations when utilizing OSINT, ensuring that their methods comply with regulations and respect privacy rights.

OSINT has become an essential tool for journalists in their pursuit of truth and accountability. By leveraging publicly available information, reporters can enhance their investigative capabilities, verify sources, and uncover stories that may otherwise remain hidden. The case studies presented illustrate the transformative impact of OSINT in journalism, showcasing its role in fostering transparency and informed public discourse. As the media landscape continues to evolve, the effective use of OSINT will remain critical in addressing challenges and upholding the integrity of journalism.

Chapter 12: Becoming a Cyber Sleuth: Careers and Skills in OSINT

Chapter 12, Becoming a Cyber Sleuth: Careers and Skills in OSINT, serves as a comprehensive guide for readers interested in pursuing a career in open-source intelligence. This chapter outlines the core competencies and skills essential for success in the field, including analytical thinking, digital literacy, and technical proficiency with OSINT tools and methodologies. Readers will learn about various career paths available in OSINT, ranging from law enforcement and cybersecurity to corporate intelligence and journalism. The chapter also discusses the importance of continuous learning, certifications, and professional development resources to stay updated in this rapidly evolving landscape. Additionally, it highlights the growing demand for OSINT professionals and offers practical advice on building a personal brand and networking within the community. By the end of this chapter, readers will be inspired and equipped to embark on their journey as cyber sleuths, ready to contribute meaningfully to the field of open-source intelligence.

12.1 Developing Core Skills for OSINT: Important skills for OSINT, from data analysis to threat intelligence.

Open Source Intelligence (OSINT) has become an indispensable aspect of various fields, including cybersecurity, law enforcement, journalism, and corporate security. The increasing demand for skilled professionals in this area necessitates a robust set of competencies that can effectively gather, analyze, and interpret publicly available data. This section outlines the core skills essential for anyone looking to excel in OSINT, ranging from data analysis to threat intelligence.

1. Critical Thinking and Analytical Skills

Definition: Critical thinking is the ability to analyze information objectively and make reasoned judgments. Analytical skills refer to the capacity to interpret data, identify patterns, and draw meaningful conclusions.

Importance: In the context of OSINT, critical thinking enables practitioners to evaluate the credibility of sources and the relevance of information. Strong analytical skills help them synthesize vast amounts of data into actionable insights.

Application: For instance, when investigating a cybersecurity breach, an OSINT analyst must assess various data points—such as IP addresses, domain registrations, and social media activity—to identify potential threat actors and understand their motivations.

2. Research Skills

Definition: Research skills involve the ability to systematically gather, evaluate, and synthesize information from various sources.

Importance: OSINT professionals must be proficient in locating and extracting relevant data from a multitude of sources, including public records, social media platforms, and news articles.

Application: A journalist, for example, might use research skills to uncover details about a public figure's background, scrutinizing everything from social media profiles to online publications to verify claims made in an article.

3. Familiarity with OSINT Tools and Technologies

Definition: This skill encompasses knowledge of various tools and software designed for OSINT gathering and analysis, such as Maltego, Shodan, and social media monitoring tools.

Importance: Understanding how to effectively utilize these tools can significantly enhance the efficiency and effectiveness of OSINT operations.

Application: A cybersecurity analyst might use Maltego to map relationships between different entities involved in a cyber threat, providing visual insights that can aid in threat mitigation.

4. Data Analysis and Visualization

Definition: Data analysis involves the interpretation of collected data, while data visualization is the graphical representation of this data to facilitate understanding.

Importance: The ability to analyze and visualize data is crucial for turning complex information into digestible insights that can inform decision-making.

Application: In corporate security, an OSINT analyst might compile data from various sources into visual formats, such as graphs or charts, to highlight trends in public sentiment about a brand or to illustrate the connections between different threats.

5. Understanding of Cybersecurity Principles

Definition: This skill involves knowledge of fundamental cybersecurity concepts, such as threat modeling, risk assessment, and incident response.

Importance: A solid grounding in cybersecurity principles is vital for OSINT professionals, especially those focused on identifying and mitigating threats.

Application: An OSINT practitioner working in cybersecurity may analyze data to identify vulnerabilities in a company's online presence, recommending proactive measures to safeguard against potential attacks.

6. Communication Skills

Definition: Communication skills involve the ability to convey information clearly and effectively, both in writing and verbally.

Importance: OSINT professionals must be able to present their findings in a manner that is understandable to various stakeholders, including management, law enforcement, or the general public.

Application: A journalist using OSINT must write compelling and accurate articles that effectively communicate the findings of their investigations, ensuring that their audience comprehends the implications of the information presented.

7. Ethical and Legal Awareness

Definition: This skill involves understanding the legal frameworks and ethical considerations that govern the collection and use of open-source information.

Importance: OSINT professionals must navigate privacy laws and ethical guidelines to ensure their work complies with regulations and respects individual rights.

Application: For example, when gathering information about a subject for a news story, a journalist must ensure that their methods do not infringe upon privacy laws or ethical standards, maintaining credibility and integrity in their reporting.

8. Technical Skills

Definition: Technical skills encompass a range of competencies related to using software, coding, and understanding network structures.

Importance: Familiarity with programming languages like Python or R can enhance data gathering and analysis capabilities. Technical skills can also help in automating repetitive tasks.

Application: An OSINT analyst might use Python scripts to scrape data from websites or to automate data analysis processes, thereby improving efficiency and allowing for deeper insights.

9. Networking and Relationship Building

Definition: This skill involves creating and maintaining professional relationships that can enhance information sharing and collaboration.

Importance: Building a network of contacts in relevant fields can provide access to valuable insights and resources that enhance OSINT efforts.

Application: A corporate security analyst might connect with law enforcement or other corporate security professionals to share intelligence about emerging threats, benefiting from collective knowledge and resources.

10. Cultural and Contextual Awareness

Definition: This skill involves understanding cultural nuances and the context surrounding the information being analyzed.

Importance: Context is critical in interpreting data accurately. Awareness of cultural dynamics can help OSINT professionals avoid misinterpretation and make more informed decisions.

Application: For instance, when reporting on global events, a journalist must consider cultural factors that could influence public sentiment and behavior, ensuring a nuanced and informed approach to their reporting.

As OSINT continues to evolve and become increasingly integral to various sectors, developing these core skills is essential for professionals aspiring to excel in this field. By cultivating critical thinking, research proficiency, technical aptitude, and ethical awareness, individuals can significantly enhance their effectiveness in gathering and analyzing open-source information. Whether in journalism, cybersecurity, or corporate security, these skills equip professionals to uncover valuable insights, verify information, and contribute to informed decision-making in their respective fields. As the landscape of open-source intelligence grows, continuous learning and adaptation will be key to staying ahead in this dynamic environment.

12.2 Certifications and Resources for OSINT: Overview of certifications, courses, and communities for OSINT practitioners.

As Open Source Intelligence (OSINT) continues to gain prominence across various fields, the demand for skilled practitioners has surged. To stand out in this competitive landscape, obtaining certifications, completing relevant courses, and engaging with professional communities are essential strategies for OSINT professionals. This section provides an overview of the key certifications, educational resources, and community platforms that can aid practitioners in their OSINT journey.

1. Certifications in OSINT

Certifications serve as formal recognition of an individual's skills and knowledge in OSINT practices. They can enhance career prospects and validate expertise to employers and clients.

1.1 Certified OSINT Professional (COSINTP)

- **Offered by**: The Open Source Intelligence Training Institute (OSITI)
- **Overview**: This certification focuses on the core principles and techniques of OSINT. It covers various topics, including data collection methods, analytical skills, and ethical considerations.
- **Benefits**: Earning this certification demonstrates a professional's commitment to OSINT practices and equips them with practical skills for immediate application in their work.

1.2 Certified Information Systems Security Professional (CISSP)

- **Offered by**: (ISC)²
- **Overview**: While not exclusively focused on OSINT, the CISSP certification includes a comprehensive understanding of information security practices, which are critical for OSINT professionals, particularly in cybersecurity contexts.
- **Benefits**: This globally recognized certification provides a strong foundation in security principles and practices, enhancing an OSINT professional's credibility in the field of cybersecurity.

1.3 GIAC Cyber Threat Intelligence (GCTI)

- **Offered by**: Global Information Assurance Certification (GIAC)
- **Overview**: This certification focuses on the collection and analysis of cyber threat intelligence, which overlaps significantly with OSINT practices. It includes topics such as threat modeling, analysis techniques, and reporting.
- **Benefits**: GCTI certification equips professionals with the skills needed to understand and respond to cyber threats effectively, making it valuable for those working in cybersecurity or intelligence roles.

1.4 Open Source Intelligence Training (OSINT)

- **Offered by**: Various organizations and institutions
- **Overview**: Many training providers offer OSINT-specific courses and certifications. These programs often cover fundamental concepts, advanced techniques, and practical applications of OSINT.
- **Benefits**: Completing such courses can enhance a professional's knowledge base and skill set, preparing them for real-world OSINT challenges.

2. Online Courses and Learning Platforms

Numerous online platforms offer courses tailored to OSINT practitioners, catering to various skill levels and interests.

2.1 Coursera

Overview: Coursera partners with universities and organizations to offer a wide range of courses, including topics related to data analysis, cybersecurity, and OSINT.

Recommended Courses:

- "Introduction to Cyber Attacks" by NYU
- "Data Analysis and Visualization" by Wesleyan University

Benefits: Flexible learning options allow practitioners to learn at their own pace, and courses often provide certificates upon completion.

2.2 Udemy

Overview: Udemy features a plethora of courses on OSINT tools and techniques, ranging from beginner to advanced levels.

Recommended Courses:

- "OSINT: Open Source Intelligence for Beginners"
- "Maltego for Open Source Intelligence Gathering"

Benefits: Udemy offers lifetime access to courses, enabling learners to revisit material as needed and stay updated on new techniques.

2.3 Pluralsight

Overview: Pluralsight offers specialized courses in cybersecurity and data analysis, including OSINT techniques.

Recommended Courses:

- "Gathering Intelligence from Open Sources"
- "Understanding and Using OSINT Tools"

Benefits: The platform features hands-on learning experiences, allowing practitioners to apply concepts in real-time scenarios.

2.4 SANS Institute

Overview: SANS is a well-respected provider of cybersecurity training and certifications, including OSINT-related content.

Recommended Courses:

- "FOR578: Cyber Threat Intelligence"

- "SEC487: Open-Source Intelligence (OSINT) Gathering and Analysis"

Benefits: SANS courses are often led by industry experts, providing high-quality instruction and insights into current practices.

3. Books and Publications

Reading relevant literature can deepen understanding and provide fresh perspectives on OSINT practices.

3.1 "Open Source Intelligence Techniques" by Michael Bazzell

- **Overview**: This book serves as a comprehensive guide to OSINT, covering techniques, tools, and best practices.
- **Benefits**: It includes practical examples and case studies, making it an invaluable resource for both beginners and experienced practitioners.

3.2 "The New New Thing: A Silicon Valley Story" by Michael Lewis

- **Overview**: While not solely focused on OSINT, this book offers insights into the world of technology and information, highlighting the importance of data in modern society.
- **Benefits**: It provides context for understanding the broader implications of data collection and analysis.

4. Professional Communities and Forums

Engaging with professional communities allows OSINT practitioners to share knowledge, collaborate, and stay updated on industry trends.

4.1 The OSINT Curious Project

- **Overview**: This community focuses on sharing resources, tools, and techniques related to OSINT. It features podcasts, blogs, and webinars.
- **Benefits**: Practitioners can learn from experts, participate in discussions, and access a wealth of information on OSINT topics.

4.2 r/OSINT Subreddit

- **Overview**: The OSINT subreddit on Reddit serves as a community for practitioners to share insights, resources, and experiences.
- **Benefits**: Users can ask questions, seek advice, and discuss emerging trends and tools in the OSINT field.

4.3 LinkedIn Groups

- **Overview**: Various LinkedIn groups focus on OSINT, cybersecurity, and intelligence analysis. These groups facilitate networking and knowledge sharing among professionals.
- **Benefits**: Engaging in discussions and connecting with peers can lead to collaboration opportunities and access to exclusive resources.

4.4 Local Meetups and Conferences

- **Overview**: Many cities host meetups and conferences focused on OSINT and related fields, providing opportunities for networking and professional development.
- **Benefits**: Attending these events allows practitioners to meet industry leaders, share experiences, and stay informed about the latest developments in OSINT.

As the demand for OSINT expertise grows, practitioners must seek out relevant certifications, courses, and community resources to enhance their skills and knowledge. By pursuing formal recognition through certifications, engaging in continuous learning through online courses, and connecting with professional communities, OSINT practitioners can position themselves as valuable assets in their respective fields. With a commitment to ongoing education and networking, individuals can stay ahead in the rapidly evolving landscape of open source intelligence, contributing effectively to their organizations and the broader industry.

12.3 Future Trends and Challenges in OSINT: Emerging issues in OSINT, from AI impacts to ethical concerns.

Open Source Intelligence (OSINT) is continuously evolving, driven by advancements in technology, changing societal norms, and emerging threats. As OSINT becomes more integral to cybersecurity, law enforcement, corporate security, and journalism, it faces a myriad of future trends and challenges. This section explores the key issues on the horizon, particularly focusing on the impacts of artificial intelligence (AI), data privacy, ethical concerns, and the evolving landscape of information availability.

1. The Impact of Artificial Intelligence

1.1 Automation of OSINT Processes

- **Trend Overview**: AI and machine learning are increasingly being integrated into OSINT processes, enabling automation of data collection, analysis, and reporting.
- **Implications**: While automation can enhance efficiency and reduce human error, it may also lead to an over-reliance on algorithms, potentially resulting in biases if not properly calibrated. The ability of AI to process vast amounts of data rapidly can uncover patterns and insights that human analysts may overlook, but it raises concerns about the validity of the conclusions drawn.

1.2 Enhanced Analytical Capabilities

- **Trend Overview**: AI tools can analyze and visualize complex data sets, offering advanced analytical capabilities that were previously unattainable.
- **Implications**: AI-driven analytics can provide deeper insights into trends and anomalies in open-source data. However, the black-box nature of some AI systems can hinder transparency, making it challenging for analysts to understand how conclusions were reached, thereby impacting the credibility of the findings.

1.3 AI-Generated Content

- **Trend Overview**: The rise of AI-generated content presents both opportunities and challenges in the OSINT field.
- **Implications**: On one hand, AI can generate useful content for OSINT analysis, such as automated summaries of reports or articles. On the other hand, it also increases the prevalence of misinformation and fake news, complicating the task of verifying sources and information accuracy. Analysts must develop new skills to discern genuine content from AI-generated or manipulated information.

2. Data Privacy and Regulatory Challenges

2.1 Evolving Privacy Laws

- **Trend Overview**: As public awareness of data privacy grows, legislation surrounding the collection and use of open-source information is becoming more stringent. Laws such as the General Data Protection Regulation (GDPR) in Europe have set high standards for data protection.

- **Implications**: OSINT practitioners must navigate these complex regulations, which may limit their ability to gather and use certain types of data. Compliance with privacy laws will require ongoing education and adaptation to ensure that OSINT practices do not infringe on individuals' rights.

2.2 Ethical Data Collection

- **Trend Overview**: The ethical implications of data collection practices are under increasing scrutiny, particularly concerning the impact on individuals' privacy and rights.
- **Implications**: OSINT professionals must grapple with the moral responsibilities of their work. This includes making decisions about what information to collect and how to use it, balancing the need for intelligence against the potential for harm. Developing clear ethical guidelines will be essential in maintaining trust and credibility in OSINT practices.

2.3 Transparency and Accountability

- **Trend Overview**: There is a growing demand for transparency and accountability in how OSINT is conducted, especially in law enforcement and intelligence communities.
- **Implications**: Practitioners will need to implement measures that ensure their processes are transparent and that they can be held accountable for their actions. This may involve establishing clear protocols for data collection, analysis, and reporting, as well as providing mechanisms for oversight and review.

3. Misinformation and Disinformation Challenges

3.1 The Proliferation of Fake News

- **Trend Overview**: The rise of social media has accelerated the spread of misinformation and disinformation, complicating the OSINT landscape.
- **Implications**: OSINT practitioners must develop sophisticated methods to identify and counter false information. This requires not only technical skills to analyze data but also critical thinking and media literacy to discern credible sources from unreliable ones. The battle against misinformation will be an ongoing challenge, necessitating constant vigilance and adaptation.

3.2 Psychological Operations and Information Warfare

- **Trend Overview**: State and non-state actors increasingly use information warfare techniques to manipulate public perception and achieve strategic objectives.
- **Implications**: OSINT professionals will need to be adept at recognizing and analyzing psychological operations (PSYOP) and the narratives being pushed by various actors. Understanding the motivations behind misinformation campaigns will be critical in developing effective countermeasures.

4. Evolving Sources of Open Data

4.1 Increasing Data Availability

- **Trend Overview**: The amount of data available from open sources continues to grow exponentially, thanks to the proliferation of digital communication and social media platforms.
- **Implications**: While this wealth of data presents opportunities for more comprehensive OSINT analysis, it also creates challenges in terms of data overload. Practitioners must develop effective strategies to filter and prioritize relevant information while avoiding analysis paralysis.

4.2 The Role of Emerging Technologies

- **Trend Overview**: Technologies such as blockchain, IoT (Internet of Things), and mobile devices are changing the way data is generated and shared.
- **Implications**: OSINT practitioners will need to adapt to these changes, developing new techniques for gathering intelligence from decentralized and distributed data sources. The ability to analyze data from IoT devices, for example, will open up new avenues for intelligence gathering but also raises concerns about privacy and security.

5. Skill Development and Professionalization

5.1 Need for Continuous Learning

- **Trend Overview**: As the landscape of OSINT continues to evolve, the need for ongoing education and skill development becomes increasingly important.
- **Implications**: OSINT professionals must stay updated on emerging trends, tools, and technologies to remain effective. This may involve pursuing certifications,

attending workshops, and participating in professional communities to exchange knowledge and best practices.

5.2 Professionalization of the Field

- **Trend Overview**: As OSINT gains recognition as a distinct discipline, there is a growing push for the professionalization of the field, including standardizing training and certification processes.
- **Implications**: This movement can enhance the credibility of OSINT as a practice and promote ethical standards across the industry. However, it also presents challenges in terms of establishing universal standards that accommodate the diverse applications of OSINT across various sectors.

The future of OSINT is shaped by an array of trends and challenges, from the transformative impacts of AI to the ethical dilemmas surrounding data collection and privacy. As practitioners navigate this dynamic landscape, they must adapt to evolving technologies, societal expectations, and regulatory frameworks. Addressing these challenges will require a commitment to continuous learning, ethical practice, and collaboration within the OSINT community. By staying informed and proactive, OSINT professionals can ensure that they remain effective and relevant in an ever-changing environment, leveraging open-source data to provide valuable insights and intelligence in various fields.

OSINT: The Ultimate Handbook for Cyber Sleuths is an essential guide to the art and science of open-source intelligence. Designed for investigators, cybersecurity professionals, journalists, and enthusiasts, this book demystifies the methods, tools, and ethical principles that transform public data into actionable insights.

From foundational concepts to advanced techniques, each chapter empowers readers to navigate the vast realm of open data—whether analyzing social media activity, uncovering hidden connections between domains, or utilizing geolocation tools. Real-world case studies and practical exercises bring each topic to life, offering readers a hands-on experience in tackling cyber threats, verifying information, and uncovering digital evidence.

Whether you're a seasoned cyber sleuth or just beginning your journey, OSINT: The Ultimate Handbook for Cyber Sleuths equips you with the knowledge, skills, and ethical considerations necessary to excel in the ever-evolving field of OSINT. This is more than just a handbook; it's your trusted guide to unlocking the full power of open-source intelligence in a complex, interconnected world.